In the Running

Karen Zeinert

Twenty-First Century Books   Brookfield, Connecticut

Cover photographs courtesy of PhotoDisc
(American flag) and AP/Wide World Photos

Photographs courtesy of the Library of Congress: pp. 8, 12 (top), 16,
19, 27, 36, 43; AP/Wide World Photos: pp. 12 (bottom), 46, 47, 51, 74,
90, 97; © Corbis: p. 25; Brown Brothers: pp. 28–29, 80; State Historical
Society of Wisconsin: pp. 31 (# Whi (X3) 42036), 87 (# Whi (X3) 53420);
© Bettmann/Corbis: pp. 33, 41; Wyoming State Archives, Department of
State Parks and Cultural Resources: p. 57; Texas State Library
& Archives Commission: p. 58; Douglas County Museum:
p. 62 (#N1884); Franklin D. Roosevelt Library: p. 78

Library of Congress Cataloging-in-Publication Data

Zeinert, Karen.
Women in politics : in the running / Karen Zeinert.
p. cm.
Includes bibliographical references and index.
Summary: Examines the contributions women have made at every
level of American politics throughout the history of the United States,
as well as the struggles they have encountered.
ISBN 0-7613-2253-1 (lib. bdg.)
Women in politics—juvenile literature.
[1. Women in politics.] I. Title.
HQ1236 .Z445 2002
320'.082—dc21   2001052253

Published by Twenty-First Century Books
A Division of The Millbrook Press, Inc.
2 Old New Milford Road
Brookfield, Connecticut 06804

When people ask me why I am running as a woman,
I always answer, "What choice do I have?"
—Patricia Schroeder, U.S. representative 1973–1997

CONTENTS

CHAPTER 1 ∞ Turnabout 9

CHAPTER 2 ∞ The Battle Begins 15

CHAPTER 3 ∞ The Battle Intensifies 23

CHAPTER 4 ∞ A Woman's Place Is in
the House . . . and Senate 39

CHAPTER 5 ∞ On the Local Scene 55

CHAPTER 6 ∞ In the Courtroom 65

CHAPTER 7 ∞ Presidential Advisers 77

CHAPTER 8 ∽ Running for the Highest Office 85

CHAPTER 9 ∽ The Future 95

∽ Timeline 99

∽ Notes 103

∽ Bibliography 105

∽ Further Reading 107

∽ Index 109

WOMEN IN POLITICS

CHAPTER 1

Turnabout

Many young people believe that all the privileges, all the freedom, all the enjoyments which woman now possesses always were hers. They have no idea of how every single inch of ground that she stands upon today has been gained by the hard work of some little handful of women of the past.

—Susan B. Anthony, suffragist

On June 17, 1873, Susan Brownell Anthony was the center of attention in a small courtroom in Canandaigua, New York. A well-known crusader who had dedicated her life to social reform, Anthony had been a supporter of the antislavery movement, a founder of the Daughters of Temperance (an organization devoted to curbing alcoholism), and, believing that women should be able to vote, a leader in the women's suffrage movement. Although her participation in the first two causes sometimes created controversy, it was her commitment to suffrage that got her into serious trouble: She had been arrested after illegally casting a ballot in the 1872 presidential election.

Since then, speculation about the outcome of Anthony's trial had set tongues wagging in Canandaigua. So early on the morning of June 17, curious townspeople—joined by ex-president Millard Fillmore, several U.S. senators, and dozens of Anthony's supporters—had rushed to the courthouse to get the few seats available.

After what seemed like a long wait, Judge Ward Hunt finally entered the room, and the spectators leaned forward in great anticipation, hoping for an action-packed, precedent-setting trial. Few, however, could have predicted the strange events that would follow.

Richard Crowley, the prosecutor, told the jury that the case against Anthony was open and shut. Plainly put, he said, the law denied women in New York State—as it did in all states then—the right to vote. Even so, after Anthony had found sympathetic poll workers, she had cast a ballot anyway. In addition, she had encouraged at least twelve other women to follow her example. The court, Crowley concluded, had little choice but to find the defendant guilty as charged and punish her to the full extent of the law. Otherwise, Anthony—and who knew how many other women?—might vote again.

Henry R. Selden, Anthony's lawyer, presented a spirited defense that involved a new interpretation of the U.S. Constitution's Fourteenth Amendment. This amendment, written at the end of the Civil War, stated, among other things, that anyone born in the United States was a citizen. It also contained a section that made it illegal for a state to treat its citizens differently from one another. The purpose of the first section was to grant 4 million newly freed slaves citizenship, and the other section was included to make sure that states didn't take away the ex-slaves' new legal status.

With a copy of the amendment in hand, Selden told a wide-eyed jury that the amendment applied to Susan B. Anthony as well. Since she was born in the United States, she was a citizen. This meant that New York had to grant her the same rights that New York's men had, including the right to cast a ballot. When his client voted, Selden argued, she had simply exercised one of her constitutionally given rights, and therefore she should not be punished. He concluded by saying that Miss Anthony was most eager to take the stand to explain her actions.

But to Selden's surprise, Judge Hunt refused to let the defendant explain anything. Instead, he pulled a piece of paper from his pocket and read a prepared statement. He told the jury that Anthony had broken the law, no matter what her reasons were—a new interpretation, indeed!—and he insisted that the jury find her guilty. Selden, flabbergasted by the judge's outrageous behavior, objected first that Hunt had judged Anthony long before he had heard a single word of testimony and then that he had told a jury what to think. Hunt, for obvious reasons, overruled Selden's objections.

The next day Anthony was sentenced in the crowded courtroom. Before announcing her punishment, Judge Hunt asked her if she had anything to say. This was Anthony's chance to speak her mind, and she proceeded without a moment's hesitation.

> I have many things to say. . . .[Y]ou have trampled underfoot every vital principle of our government. My natural rights, my civil rights, my political rights are all alike ignored. . . .I am degraded from the status of a citizen to that of a subject; and not only myself individually, but all of my sex are, by your honor's verdict, doomed to political subjection under this so-called Republican government.[1]

Judge Hunt, who was expecting an apology, was stunned by Anthony's reply. As soon as he realized that she was anything but sorry for what she had done, he pounded with his gavel and demanded silence. Well aware that continuing to speak for any length of time would only make her situation worse, Anthony let loose a few more well-aimed barbs, then did as she was told. When she stopped speaking, Judge Hunt announced her sentence. She was to pay a fine of $100.

Although not invited to do so—Hunt wasn't about to make the same mistake twice—Anthony spoke again. "May it please your honor, I shall never pay a dollar of your unjust penalty."[2] No one in the courtroom doubted that she meant exactly what she said.

Society's perceptions toward women's involvement in the political world have changed dramatically since the time of Susan B. Anthony's unsuccessful attempt to vote in 1872. Can you imagine a cartoon like the one on the right being published today about a woman involved in politics, such as Elizabeth Dole (below, with her husband, former senator Bob Dole), who announced her bid for president in 1999?

In sharp contrast to Susan B. Anthony's plight in 1873, in early 1999, Elizabeth Dole announced her candidacy for the presidency of the United States. Few people were shocked by her decision to run, nor did they question her right to do this, for not only could women vote, but they had expanded their role in the political arena over the years, running for any position of their choice, even the highest office in the land. How could such a dramatic turnabout have taken place? What effect did it have in the political arena? And just as important, what likely effect will women's participation in American politics have on our country's future? The answers lie in the text that follows.

CHAPTER 2

The Battle Begins

The men say we have no business with [politics], it is not in our sphere! I won't have it thought that because we are the weaker sex as to bodily strength . . . we are capable of nothing more than minding the dairy and visiting the poultry-house.
—Eliza Wilkinson, Yonge's Island, South Carolina, 1774

Steely determination on the part of some American women to play at least a small role in politics goes back to the 1770s, when American colonists were trying to force King George III of England to treat his colonial subjects better. One method the colonists used to get the king's attention was a massive boycott. Colonial leaders told women to stop buying English products and instead weave their own cloth, make their own soap, and brew tea from herbs. Many did so with great enthusiasm.

But not all females were willing to simply follow orders. On October 25, 1774, fifty-one women in Edenton, North Carolina, signed a proclamation written by Penelope Barker stating that because the outcome of the conflict between the colonies and England would affect their lives, they had a duty to become directly involved in the dispute. They intended to discuss issues and decide for themselves what they would do. Eventually the women announced that they would back the boycott. They stopped drinking tea that came from Great Britain, and in remembrance of a famous tea party in Boston, their action became known as the "Edenton Tea Party."

Penelope Barker's proclamation would get little attention today. But it was generally believed then that although it was all right for women to follow orders that embroiled them in political activities, it was unladylike—and therefore unacceptable—for women to take action on their own. As a result, Barker's proclamation got quite a response, first from her shocked husband and later from newspaper readers in England. A very unflattering cartoon portraying the

The nerve of Penelope Barker and her associates in Edenton, North Carolina, to make a public proclamation about the state of affairs between the colonies and Great Britain in 1774 shocked people in the colonies and prompted this derisive British cartoon.

Edenton women as silly hussies with mile-high wigs and plunging necklines appeared in several London papers.

Although this cartoon made readers in England laugh out loud at the women's decision, the proclamation was anything but funny in the colonies. Those who supported the king were aghast at the women's stand, afraid that the British would think that all colonial women were like those in Edenton. On the other hand, the men protesting the king's actions needed all the help they could get, so they quickly endorsed Barker's stand. These men looked upon female involvement in public affairs as temporary, and they assumed that once the crisis between Great Britain and the colonies was resolved, women would again refrain from showing any interest in political matters.

But this proved to be wishful thinking on the men's part. As tension between the king and his colonies increased, many colonial men argued passionately about taxes, legislation, and most of all, representation. Colonial women overheard some of these debates, and they became more engaged in political issues than ever before. One woman wondered aloud how women could avoid becoming interested in "the most animating Subject . . . one that Concerns us all."[1]

When violence erupted between England and the colonies in April 1775, some colonial leaders began to press for more than teaching King George a lesson or two; these men wanted nothing less than independence. As more arguments for freedom from British rule were made by colonial leaders, women began to talk about freedom not only for the colonies but for themselves as well.

For more than one hundred years, colonial women had been expected to marry, raise a family, manage their homes efficiently, and above all else, obey their husbands. It was the custom of the day to treat spouses as one body. Logically, one body has one voice, and the laws of the day gave that voice to the husband. Wives could not sue, sign contracts, or own property. Actually, in some ways, wives were little more than property themselves. If a wife ran away, she could be seized and returned to her husband just as a slave might be returned to his or her owner, and like a slave, a wife could legally be beaten. Needless to say, many women considered these laws unfair, but lacking political power or expertise, they could do little except complain.

Once independence was declared on July 4, 1776, many colonial women set out to support the Revolution. Some also used the dramatic events unfolding around them to prove themselves worthy of a different role in the new nation that would surely follow. So they ran shops and farms on the home front while men were on the battlefield, volunteered to care for the wounded, and carried messages for General George Washington's troops. A few even donned men's clothing and fired at the enemy.

Although the patriots appreciated any and all help women gave during the Revolution, neither the first government nor the federal government that followed in 1789 was prepared to grant women a political voice. One proposal debated by the representatives considered allowing single or widowed women who owned property to cast a ballot (wives were supposedly represented by their husband's vote), but this did not pass. Women were simply considered unfit to vote by a majority of the men who drafted the Constitution, especially those who wished to maintain control over their wives or who thought political issues too complex for females to understand. Also, it was commonly believed then that women were morally superior to men, and some Americans thought that allowing females to become involved in politics with its sometimes rough-and-tumble ways would taint the ladies.

Thwarted in politics, most women in the late 1700s turned all their attention to running households and raising children. But some were so full of the Revolutionary spirit that they wanted to become involved in events outside their homes. These women joined organizations devoted to educating members or helping the poor. This was acceptable to the public because women were merely extending their traditional roles a bit by becoming better wives, mothers, and neighbors.

Over the years, the public became accustomed to women taking on a few tasks outside the home. Emboldened by their success and deeply concerned by numerous social problems they saw all around them, some women began to join reform efforts, especially the fledgling antislavery movement. Women were still considered morally superior, and owning slaves was regarded as a sin by many Americans. So although this raised some eyebrows, women's involvement in abolition was thought to be a worthy activity, at least in the North.

Many antislavery organizations were run by Quakers, who had long preached equality between the sexes. Women, therefore, were allowed to assume important roles in the movement, and by the late 1830s a number of female leaders had emerged, including Elizabeth Cady Stanton and Lucretia Mott. As these women took on more responsibilities, they gained valuable organizational skills that could be used to promote any cause.

Elizabeth Cady Stanton and her daughter, Harriot, in 1856

Elizabeth Cady Stanton (1815–1902)

Young Elizabeth Cady was well educated. Even though she didn't attend college, she studied difficult subjects such as Greek, Latin, and advanced mathematics in her family home in Johnstown, New York. Her father, who served in the U.S. Congress before becoming a judge, taught her some of the rudiments of the legal profession, sometimes decrying the uselessness of this teaching, since a woman had little—if any—opportunity to practice law in America in the early 1800s.

Cady's uncle, whom she adored, introduced her to the abolitionist movement. He also introduced her to Henry Brewster Stanton, a journalist and abolitionist, whom she married in 1840. They had seven children. In 1851, Elizabeth Cady Stanton met Susan B. Anthony. They formed a fast friendship and a deep commitment to the suffrage movement that lasted until Stanton's death fifty-one years later. Together they published a weekly newspaper, the *Revolution*, founded the National Woman Suffrage Association, and fought for a suffrage amendment to the U.S. Constitution. Along with Matilda Joslyn Gage, they also wrote the first three volumes of a six-volume work, *A History of Woman Suffrage*.

In her spare time, Stanton appeared before various legislative committees in New York State. She argued for legislation that would make it possible for wives to own property and to sue for divorce without automatically losing custody of their children.

Stanton even challenged the Bible. Unhappy with the way women were portrayed in some sections, she wrote a two-volume commentary, *The Woman's Bible*, to offset what she considered to be sexism. This did not endear her to some suffragists, who thought they had enough of an uphill battle without antagonizing Christian leaders along the way. Stanton, unwavering in her beliefs, took the criticism in stride.

In 1840, Stanton and Mott traveled to London to attend the World Anti-Slavery Convention. When they tried to sit with male delegates, convention leaders asked them to move. Women, they were told, were to sit behind a curtain where they could listen to the proceedings.

Humiliated by such treatment, Stanton and Mott started a new crusade: equal rights for women. After finding several hundred like-minded females in the coming years, Stanton and Mott held a meeting in Seneca Falls, New York, now known as the Seneca Falls Convention, on July 19 and 20, 1848. Besides seeking laws that would make it possible for women to own property and sign contracts, many delegates to the convention insisted that the group fight for suffrage. How, these delegates asked, could women ever achieve equality with men without being able to vote? And so the official struggle for the ballot began.

CHAPTER 3

The Battle Intensifies

How Long Must Women Wait for Liberty?
— National Woman's Party slogan

Even though the Seneca Falls Convention stirred women all across the land to action on their own behalf, events in America conspired against them. The issue of slavery garnered more and more attention in the 1850s, and abolitionist leaders now believed that their goal was within reach if they could find more volunteers to help persuade the public and the politicians that slavery was wrong. To attract more helpers, especially militant suffragists who proved to be untiring crusaders, abolitionists promised to support suffrage in the future, if women would put all their energy into ending slavery now. Many suffragists, deeply committed to freedom for all, willingly set aside their own needs and threw themselves into the antislavery movement with great zeal.

When the Civil War broke out between the North and South, suffragists pushed even harder for abolition. In 1863, Susan B. Anthony became one of the founders of the Women's Loyal National

League. Its only purpose was to secure an amendment to the Constitution that would forever outlaw slavery in the United States. In order to amend the Constitution, two-thirds of congressional legislators have to pass an amendment, and three-fourths of state legislatures must ratify (approve) it.

To push this cause, suffragists drafted petitions, stood on street corners to get signatures—each signer was asked to pay a penny if possible to help raise funds for the cause—and, with petitions in hand, lobbied congressmen. When the Thirteenth Amendment, which abolished slavery, was ratified in 1865, members dissolved the league.

Shortly after, suffragists resumed their campaign for the right of women to vote. But their efforts were hampered by at least three factors. First, abolitionists reneged on their promise. Instead of fighting to remove race *and* sex from voting restrictions, abolitionists decided to put all their efforts into securing the vote for black men. The crusaders argued that because so many Americans opposed voting rights for women, including them in a suffrage amendment would put at risk the chance to grant black men the ballot, which the public tended to favor. Women, the men said, would have to wait their turn. Understandably, suffragists considered this an outright betrayal.

Second, many suffragists were in awe of the significant gains that women had made during the Civil War. For the first time in American history, thousands of women had served as professional nurses—one woman had even worked as a doctor at the front—while thousands more had been sought out for secretarial positions in federal offices. Others had taken industrial jobs denied them before the war. Most important of all, some females would be able to keep their positions. This was very important, for many women would not have husbands to support them. More than half a million men had died in the conflict.

The dramatic changes in some women's lives as a result of the war did not sit well with many Americans, especially those who thought that a woman's place was in the home. Now, some suffragists argued, pushing for the right to vote might cause a backlash,

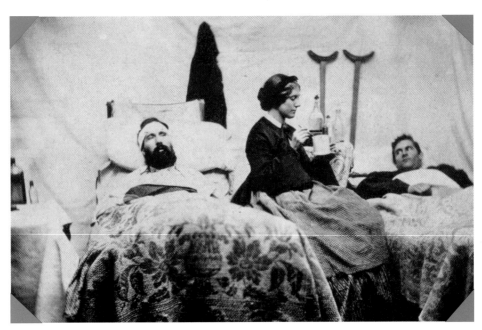

The women's suffrage movement gained momentum after the Civil War, which marked the first time in United States history that women contributed in large numbers to a national cause. The war gave them an opportunity to demonstrate their value to society as a whole. Pictured is one of thousands of nurses as she cares for wounded Union soldiers.

putting in jeopardy all that had been gained. It was best, they pleaded, to wait awhile for the ballot.

The third reason that the suffrage movement stumbled after the Civil War was another civil war of sorts; those who remained committed to the cause were deeply divided about how best to accomplish their goal. One group, the National Woman Suffrage Association, headed by Susan B. Anthony, wanted to add a suffrage amendment to the Constitution. This would take time to accomplish, and because women currently faced so many problems, for example, unfair property and divorce laws, Anthony also wanted to push for legislation that would immediately benefit females.

Another group, which called itself the American Woman Suffrage Association, was headed by Lucy Stone, who, like Anthony, was a former abolitionist. This organization focused only on the issue of suffrage. To do otherwise, Stone argued, was to risk alienating someone for each issue supported, and the suffrage movement couldn't afford to offend anyone if women were going to get the vote in Stone's lifetime.

For twenty years, members in both associations distributed pamphlets, gave speeches, and lobbied representatives. But despite their hard work, neither group made much headway. When women presented a suffrage amendment for consideration in Congress in 1876, it was greeted with poorly disguised contempt.

Frustrated, and tired of fighting each other, the two associations joined forces in 1890. Using portions of both organizations' names to satisfy all members, the new coalition was known as the National American Woman Suffrage Association (NAWSA). It was headed by Anthony.

Eventually NAWSA's leaders decided to fight for suffrage on two fronts. Some women would lobby national legislators to pass the suffrage amendment, while others, heartened by the fact that Wyoming Territory had enfranchised women, fought for the ballot in individual states. This strategy relied heavily on women who would persuade their husbands, fathers, brothers, and sons—if adults—to pressure local politicians, especially those who wanted to be reelected, to change state voting laws. Suffrage leaders hoped that when Congress finally passed the amendment, there would be enough states that had already granted women the right to vote to make ratification a sure thing. This was called the "winning plan."

Yet despite an all-out drive by NAWSA, little progress was made in the next ten years on any front. Congress refused to seriously consider a suffrage amendment, and only Wyoming, Utah, Colorado, and Idaho granted women the right to vote.

But the tide began to turn in the suffragists' favor in the early 1900s. When Americans looked around then, they saw many problems: dangerous working conditions; poverty; child labor; immigrants crowded into tiny, dirty apartments; and corrupt politicians. Although these were not entirely new conditions, many Americans were now ready to roll up their sleeves and change America. Historians call this period the Progressive Era.

In 1869, Wyoming, then a territory, granted women the right to vote, making Wyoming women the first in the nation to have this right. This 1888 scene from Wyoming shows what must have been a curiosity to people around the United States: women voting. Wyoming territory officially became a state in 1890.

Building upon the new spirit that was sweeping the land, suffragists worked harder than ever for their cause. They argued that not only would giving women the ballot be just, but, because of their moral superiority, women could help clean up politics, a promise that attracted a good deal of attention from the public.

At the same time, the National American Woman Suffrage Association's membership changed. Younger women, some of whom had worked with suffragists in England when they had successfully won the vote, returned to America to influence, then lead, the movement. In addition, instead of trying to attract only middle-class, well-educated members, leaders reached out to working-class women, arguing that with the ballot, female laborers could elect representatives who could pass legislation that would improve conditions in the workplace. Not only did these laborers join in large numbers, but, hardened by ten-hour workdays and numerous disputes that had sometimes ended in strikes, working women proved to be fearless crusaders for the ballot.

Suffragist leaders, prodded by younger members, also pushed to make their cause more visible. More women than ever before lobbied legislators on both the national and local level, gave speeches, presented petitions, and held huge parades—a 1913 spectacle in Washington, D.C., featured 8,000 marchers—that the press loved to

cover. The results were astounding. In 1905 the National American Woman Suffrage Association had 17,000 members; eleven years later, its membership numbered 2 million.

But just when everything seemed to be going well, the association split. A group of women led by Alice Paul was determined to force the issue of suffrage. Tired of waiting and certain that a lady-like campaign for the vote, which had long been the approach, would never succeed, Paul argued for more militant tactics. Carrie Chapman Catt, then the head of NAWSA, believed that confrontation would cause the association to lose public support. She insisted on wooing legislators. Unwilling to accept this approach, Paul and her followers formed the National Woman's Party (NWP) in 1916.

With the Capitol dome in the background, marchers set off down Pennsylvania Avenue in Washington, D.C. Although the photo is undated, it quite possibly pictures part of the huge women's suffrage parade of 1913.

Carrie Chapman Catt (1859–1947)

Carrie Chapman Catt, born Carrie Lane, spent most of her youth in Iowa. After graduation from high school—in three years—she decided to attend college. Because her father could not pay for her education, she took a teaching position to earn money for her tuition. (Unlike today, high-school graduates then could teach if they passed rigorous examinations.) In 1877, she entered Iowa State College at Ames, where, after receiving her degree, she hoped to study law.

To pay for her schooling, Carrie again sought work, this time accepting a position as a school principal in Mason City, Iowa. There she met Leo Chapman, the editor and publisher of the local newspaper. They were married in 1885.

Mrs. Chapman became her husband's assistant editor. At the time, women in Iowa were just beginning to press for suffrage.

After writing several articles about this issue, she joined the crusade for the ballot. Shortly after, Leo Chapman died.

Five years later, Carrie married George Catt, a strong supporter of women's rights. George Catt's sizable income made it possible for his wife to travel all over America, giving speeches and raising funds. In the process, Catt made a name for herself. In 1900 she was elected president of the National American Woman Suffrage Association, taking over when Susan B. Anthony retired.

When George Catt became seriously ill in 1904, Carrie left the organization to care for him. After his death, she resumed her suffrage efforts in New York State. In 1915 she was again elected president of NAWSA, and she served until the Nineteenth Amendment was passed. She then played a leading role in the formation of the League of Women Voters.

The following year, the United States entered World War I, and many women offered their services as nurses, doctors, secretaries for the armed forces, laborers in war industries, and volunteers at

Carrie Chapman Catt in 1917

soldiers' canteens. Catt encouraged women to volunteer—she even offered the services of the members of NAWSA—believing that once Americans saw how important women were to the war effort, they would finally agree that women should be given the ballot.

Alice Paul believed, however, that until women had the vote, they should not support America's entry into the war. Instead, Paul argued, NWP members should seize this opportunity and wage war on the home front for the ballot, making it perfectly clear that as soon as they were enfranchised, they would help defeat America's enemies.

Alice Paul, born in Moorestown, New Jersey, to Quaker parents, was a well-educated, determined young woman. After receiving advanced degrees in social work from the University of Pennsylvania, she went to England to continue her studies.

Deeply devoted to equal rights for women, she joined the British suffrage movement in 1906. These suffragists took a very public stand. British leaders, hoping to frighten the women into quitting their campaign, arrested more than a thousand demonstrators. The prisoners drew attention to their cause by going on hunger strikes. Paul was arrested three times in England, and like the rest of the demonstrators, was force-fed.

In 1909, Alice Paul returned to the United States, where she quickly became a leader in NAWSA. Believing that women had to do more than *ask* for the vote, Paul eventually left the association and started the National Woman's Party. Using techniques learned in England, especially holding parades and picketing leaders, Paul taught members how to draw attention to their cause and how to embarrass their enemies.

After the Nineteenth Amendment was passed, Paul continued her struggle for equality. She spearheaded the drive for the Equal Rights Amendment (ERA), which, if passed, would have given women the same rights men had, including equal pay for equal work, more opportunities for higher education, and the opportunity to hold jobs then limited to men. In December 1923, this amendment was introduced in Congress. U.S. legislators did not take the amendment seriously, and it wasn't passed until 1972, and then only after being reintroduced many times. The states had ten years to ratify it, but by 1982, only thirty-five of the thirty-eight states needed had done so. Paul's amendment never became part of the Constitution.

Alice Paul stands on the balcony of the National Woman's Party headquarters in Washington, D.C., in September 1920. She and other party members were rehearsing for a demonstration to be held when Tennessee ratified the Nineteenth Amendment.

Holding the politicians in office responsible for the suffragists' predicament—after all, these men had the power to change the situation—members of the National Woman's Party zeroed in on political leaders, especially President Woodrow Wilson. NWP leaders began by presenting their case to the president. How, they asked, could the president lead America into war in order to defend democracy abroad, as he had so eloquently stated, yet at the same time refuse to grant women democracy at home? When Wilson refused to take action on the suffrage issue, as many as a thousand women a day picketed the White House. Eventually scuffles broke out between pickets and spectators who came for no other purpose than to heckle the women; before the dust settled, more than a hundred NWP members had been arrested.

To demonstrate their deep commitment to the cause, imprisoned NWP women went on a hunger strike. In order to keep these women from starving to death and becoming martyrs, officials force-fed them. Revolting images of funnels jammed into women's mouths or long tubes forced down their throats and then flooded with liquid flashed through Americans' minds, creating widespread sympathy and support for both the prisoners and their mission.

On January 10, 1918, the suffrage amendment, now called the Susan B. Anthony Amendment in honor of its originator, who had died in 1906, was reintroduced in the House of Representatives. Despite powerful opposition and various attempts to keep the amendment stalled in committee meetings so that it would never be debated in the House, highly vocal representatives pushed for a fair hearing. A heated debate followed, and the amendment finally received the required two-thirds vote to pass.

The Senate, however, wasn't in a hurry. It took more than a year to debate the issue. This chamber finally passed the amendment in June 1919.

The finished version of the amendment was short and simple. The first paragraph consisted of one sentence: "The right of citizens of the United States to vote shall not be denied or abridged by the United States or by any state on account of sex." The second paragraph, again only one sentence long, contained eleven words: "Congress shall have power to enforce this Article by appropriate legislation."[1]

Thirty-six states had to ratify the amendment before it could go into effect. To increase the chances of this happening, both the National American Woman Suffrage Association and the National

Woman's Party worked ceaselessly. Arguing for simple justice, members lobbied local legislators until the officials and suffragists were exhausted. Their hard work paid off. On August 26, 1920, Tennessee, the last state needed, ratified the Nineteenth Amendment. This successfully ended a long battle for suffrage during which, as Carrie Chapman Catt and Nettie Rogers Shuler wrote in a book about the struggle for suffrage,

> Hundreds of women gave the accumulated possibilities of an entire lifetime, thousands gave years of their lives, hundreds of thousands gave constant interest and such aid as they could. It was a continuous, seemingly endless, chain of activity. Young suffragists who helped forge the last links of that chain were not born when it began. Old suffragists who forged the first links were dead when it ended. It is doubtful if any man, even among suffrage men, ever realized what the suffrage struggle came to mean to women before the end was allowed in America.[2]

To help women make the most of their new right, the National American Woman Suffrage Association started the National League of Women Voters. This organization, known today simply as the League of Women Voters, held classes to teach women about the voting process and political issues that affected their lives.

Even so, not all women found it easy to vote; black females, like black males, were openly discriminated against. When the Fifteenth Amendment, which gave black men the right to vote, had been ratified in 1870, some state legislators, especially in the South, immediately set out to limit the number of blacks who could cast ballots. Some of these legislators objected to these new voters because of racial prejudice. Others regarded giving one million black men the ballot a political ploy by Republicans, who pushed the amendment through, to ensure more Republican voters in the future.

But discrimination at the polls was difficult to achieve. The Fourteenth Amendment, which went into effect in 1868, required that all citizens be treated alike. (This is the amendment that Susan B. Anthony believed granted women suffrage.) To get around

Sojourner Truth, about 1860

Before slavery was abolished, Sojourner Truth, a former slave, traveled throughout the North, passionately arguing for abolition and women's rights. Some sources state that Sojourner Truth, born Isabella Baumfree in 1797 in a Dutch colony in what is now New York State, was set free when slavery was abolished in New York in 1828; others insist that she freed herself by running away in 1826. Six feet tall and not the least bit hesitant to speak her mind, Sojourner Truth was an imposing speaker who drew large audiences. When she spoke from the floor at women's rights conventions, insisting that women should have the same rights as men, delegates paid her considerable attention. Although she could neither read nor write, Sojourner Truth's wisdom and belief in her causes won her great respect. For many years, she served as a liaison between abolitionists and suffragists.

As soon as the last of the slaves were freed in 1865, Sojourner Truth hoped that she would be able to vote, and like her white counterparts, she was incensed when only males were enfranchised by the Fifteenth Amendment five years later. Angry, determined, and militant, she encouraged black women to support the suffrage movement.

However, white suffrage leaders—then and in the coming years—were hesitant to accept the help of any blacks. White leaders were well aware of some of the public's less-than-enthusi-

astic acceptance of black male voters. In light of such feelings, suffrage leaders worried aloud about the public's reaction to petitioners who were black *and* female. Unwilling to put the movement at risk, just as the abolitionists had once been reluctant to include women when fighting for the Fifteenth Amendment, many members discouraged black women from joining their organizations.

Rejected but unwilling to give up, blacks eventually formed their own organizations. Ida B. Wells-Barnett, a journalist, started the Alpha Suffrage Club of Chicago in 1913. The National Association of Colored Women, a nationwide organization of black women's clubs, also supported the ballot for women. Volunteers gave speeches, raised funds, marched in parades,

and picketed the White House with members of the National Woman's Party, who were not afraid to accept the help of blacks, especially those willing to risk their personal safety for the cause.

When some white suffragists, desperate to win, actually considered adding a clause to the Nineteenth Amendment that would have limited voting rights to white women to make it more acceptable to some legislators, black suffragists were outraged. They insisted on suffrage for every female. How could any woman complain about discrimination at the ballot box, they wondered, then discriminate herself? The insistence by leaders such as Wells-Barnett on being treated as equals resulted in the eventual enfranchisement of all women— no small feat.

this amendment, some voting precincts decided to assess a poll tax. Although all voters were expected to pay this fee, the price was set so high that poor people, many of whom were black, couldn't meet the demand. Other precincts decided to give literacy tests. Here again, all who showed up on voting day were questioned so that no one could claim discrimination, but the most complicated questions were reserved for blacks, who tended to be the most poorly educated. When these methods failed, terror was used to keep voters away from the ballot box. Black men who stood up for their rights were beaten and even lynched.

Understandably, such obstacles and threats eventually convinced most blacks to give up. In 1896 there were 130,000 black males registered to vote in Louisiana; in 1904 only 1,300 were on the books. The numbers in other states were just as shocking.

But in the 1960s, brave leaders such as Martin Luther King Jr. emerged on the scene. Appalled by the high levels of black poverty and mean-spirited discrimination blacks faced every day, these leaders shouted: Enough! Just as the suffragists had argued years before, they insisted that one of the best ways to improve people's lives was to elect sympathetic legislators. Blacks, leaders argued, had to register and vote in large numbers, for the larger the number, the more sympathetic lawmakers would be. To draw attention to their struggle not only for the right to vote, but for the right to be treated as equals, blacks marched, held sit-ins, and boycotted businesses that discriminated against them. This was not easy to do. Demonstrators endured verbal and physical assaults; some were even murdered.

Eventually, though, their sacrifice paid off. In 1965 legislation was passed that made it illegal to use any means—taxes and tests included—to prevent someone from voting. Then, and only then, did all women have the opportunity to vote. The battle begun in 1848 had finally been won.

CHAPTER 4

A Woman's Place Is in the House . . . and Senate

We know from the research we've done that it makes a difference to have women in the legislature. . . .Women bring a different set of life experiences to the process, which has an impact on public policy.
—Debbie Walsh, Center for American Women and Politics

When the Nineteenth Amendment was finally ratified in August 1920, curious Americans eagerly awaited the fall election to see what effect female voters would have on the political scene. Meanwhile, a few feisty women began to dream and scheme. Why elect men to fight for women's rights and concerns, they asked, when women, who now had a chance to win, thanks to the potential support of female voters, could fight for new laws in either the U.S. House of Representatives or the Senate?

These bold women were not the first to envision female politicians. For example, in 1866, Elizabeth Cady Stanton ran for the House, arguing that although women couldn't vote, there was nothing in the Constitution to prevent them from holding office.

Because Stanton was unable to get support from any political party, she ran as an independent. Her platform included several issues, but it was women's suffrage that received the most attention, the majority of it negative. In the end, only twenty-four men cast their ballots for her.

Like Stanton, Jeannette Rankin also ran for office before the Nineteenth Amendment was passed. Rankin was born in Missoula, Montana, to wealthy parents. After graduation from college, she became a social worker, serving in some of the poorest sections of Seattle and New York, where she witnessed heartbreaking suffering and misery. Rankin's father had long been involved in local politics, and her brother had recently been elected attorney general of Montana. As soon as Montana enfranchised women, Rankin's father and brother encouraged Jeannette to run for office, arguing that, if successful, she could work on legislation that would help many poor people, especially poor children, not just the few she ministered to in the slums. In 1916 she decided to run for the House.

Believing that some voters might reject her outright because she was a woman, Rankin faced the issue head-on. She argued that having women in Congress offered special benefits. Because of their traditional roles, such as caring for children, women could bring a different perspective to the legislature. "There are hundreds of men to care for the nation's tariff and foreign policy and irrigation projects," she said. "But there isn't a single woman to look after the nation's greatest asset: its children."[1] Montanans accepted her argument. She defeated her opponent by more than 10,000 votes.

Unfortunately, Rankin lost most of her support in Montana within days after arriving in Washington in the spring of 1917. War had erupted in Europe in 1914, and the conflict had turned into a horrible conflagration involving so many nations that it was called the Great War. (Today we know it as World War I.) While Rankin was traveling to the capital, President Woodrow Wilson was preparing to ask Congress to declare war on Germany and its allies. Because Germany had engaged in naval warfare against American ships and was dangerously close to defeating Europe's democracies, many Americans supported the president.

Jeannette Rankin

But Jeannette Rankin wasn't one of them. She believed that war was morally wrong. When Wilson's request was brought before the House on April 6, Rankin voted against it.

Her vote against America's participation in the Great War, which passed by a large margin, enraged many Montanans, who considered waging battle against Germany the most important issue of the day. Now being a female became a problem. Even though forty-nine men had also voted against declaring war, Rankin was singled out for attention. She wasn't, critics sneered, "manly" enough for the job.

But all was not lost. During Rankin's first two-year term in office, she successfully argued for the passage of the suffrage amendment, which she reintroduced in the House, and she helped draft the Sheppard-Towner Maternity and Infancy Aid bill. In 1918 about sixty out of every thousand newborns died each year. (In contrast, today approximately one out of every thousand infants dies annually.) The main purpose of the Sheppard-Towner bill was to provide greater access to inexpensive medical care for new mothers and infants. It was one of the first bills of its kind in America.

Although Rankin worked hard during her two years in office and accomplished several important goals, strong feelings against her because she refused to vote for war did not go away. She lost her bid for reelection in 1918. However, many years later, she returned to the House. She was in office in 1941 when President Franklin D. Roosevelt asked Congress to enter World War II. This time Rankin was the only representative who refused to support the president, making her the only legislator in American history to vote against entering both world wars.

In the fall of 1920, Americans went to the polls to elect a new president. Warren G. Harding was the Republican candidate, and James Cox represented the Democratic party. Delegates at the Democratic convention had been so divided over whom to choose that they had to vote forty-four times before any candidate got a majority.

While there was considerable interest in what effect women would have on the outcome of the election and whether women would vote as a bloc for candidates promising to fight for women's rights, as suffragists hoped, the public had little interest in actually voting. Voter turnout was surprisingly low; only 49 percent of those eligible cast ballots, 60 percent of which were for Harding. The small number of female voters, about half of those eligible to cast a ballot, upset many suffragists.

Another factor in the 1920 fall election that upset—then horrified—suffragists was Alice Mary Robertson's successful campaign in Oklahoma for a seat in the House. Robertson, a sixty-six-year-old retired teacher and the daughter of missionaries who had minis-

Alice Mary Robertson, who horrified suffragists with her statement that men had "thrust the vote on us," in a picture taken during the 1920s

tered to Native Americans in what was then Oklahoma Territory was, like Rankin, single, well educated, and independently wealthy. Unlike Rankin, Robertson opposed suffrage for women as well as most of the causes suffragists held dear to their hearts. But since women had the vote and Robertson liked a challenge, she decided to enter politics. She said, "Men have thrust the vote on us and now I am going to see whether they mean it."[2] (Understandably, the use of the term "thrust" rankled suffragists, who had *fought* for the ballot for years.) Robertson was bold—suffragists called her brazen—and blunt. Her slogan, "I cannot be bought, I cannot be sold, I cannot be intimidated," said it all.[3]

One of Robertson's first acts in Congress was to vote against Rankin's pet project, the Sheppard-Towner bill, which had finally come to the floor for debate. She argued that it would cost more than a million dollars to implement. By Robertson's standards, this was simply too much money. The bill passed anyway.

Opposition to Robertson from suffragists grew daily, but, as in Rankin's case, it was a military issue that ended her political career. When a bill supporting bonuses for World War I soldiers was introduced in the House, Robertson spoke out against it, arguing once again that it cost too much money. Her constituents thought that bonuses were due, so Robertson became a one-term representative.

Although the next two female representatives, Winnifred Sprague Mason Huck and Mae Ella Nolan, were, like Rankin and Robertson, one-term candidates, many of the more than two hundred women who followed in the House had real staying power. Learning from their predecessors' mistakes, these women handled military issues with great care. Also, some followed their husbands into office, which gave the women greater political clout than Rankin and Robertson had enjoyed.

For example, Californian Florence P. Kahn was afforded great respect. She had been her husband's campaign aide, a position she loved dearly. When her husband died in 1924, she ran for his seat, arguing that she could continue her husband's work for the voters. This was a new take on the old belief that a husband and wife were of one mind and one voice. Voters accepted Kahn's argument, as did members of the House. Then, as now, representatives were assigned to special committees; she was asked to serve on the military affairs committee, which was formerly headed by her husband. Kahn represented California in Congress until 1937.

Another woman who had both respect and staying power was Edith Nourse Rogers, who holds the record for females for the most years of service in the House (1925–1960). She was running for her nineteenth term—at age eighty—when she died. Rogers became a representative from Massachusetts when she campaigned for her husband's seat shortly after he passed away, arguing, as Kahn had, that she could carry on her husband's work.

Rogers, who worked for the Red Cross during World War I, was deeply devoted to the military and to providing equal opportunities for women. She fought for a nationwide network of veterans' hospitals to provide the best care possible for wounded soldiers. She also fought for the right of women to serve in the military. When the United States entered World War II in 1941, Rogers introduced bills that would enable women to join the armed forces' auxiliaries. This did not endear her to some male representatives, who worried aloud about who would "do the cooking, the washing, the mending, the humble, homey tasks to which every woman has devoted herself" if women were in the armed forces.[4] Despite bitter arguments, Rogers held her ground and her bills became laws.

Within only a few years after Rogers's death, vast changes once again swept over America. The Civil Rights Movement was in full swing; women, prodded by Alice Paul, were seeking the passage of the Equal Rights Amendment; and America was once again at war. U.S. soldiers were fighting in Vietnam (1965–1973). These events deeply divided America, and the home scene in the 1960s and 1970s was turbulent, even violent, at times. To help their cause, be it peace or voting rights for blacks, more women than ever before successfully sought political power. One of the results was diversity in Congress. The House witnessed the swearing in of thirty-three women from 1960 to 1979, including Patsy Takemoto Mink, the first female Asian-American representative, and Shirley Chisholm, the first black female representative.

Unlike some of her predecessors, Patsy Mink did not follow her husband into office, and she had lots of political experience before she was elected to the House. Mink, who was a lawyer, served first in Hawaii's territorial house of representatives. When the territory became a state in 1959, she was elected to the state senate. In 1964 she won a seat in the U.S. House, where she served until 1977. She then made an unsuccessful try for a Senate seat. Mink returned to the House in 1990.

Patsy Mink has long been committed to equal opportunities for women. She is best known for her support of an amendment to the Title IX Education Act of 1972. This amendment made it illegal for schools to deny educational or athletic opportunities because of one's sex. It took years to implement, but eventually girls were offered scholastic and athletic opportunities—their own basketball

Patsy Takemoto Mink in 1997

teams, for example—that had been denied them until the amendment went into effect. In addition to providing equal opportunity, Mink has been involved with immigration, health care, and campaign-finance reform issues.

Shirley Chisholm was born in Brooklyn, New York, to immigrant parents from the West Indies. Her mother and father, who were far from wealthy, saw to it that Shirley received a college education. She eventually earned a master's degree in child education from Columbia University by attending night classes. To pay her tuition, she taught school during the day. With her husband's support, Chisholm successfully ran for a seat in the New York State Assembly in 1964. Because she loved children, she fought for more funds for elementary and secondary schools and college scholarships for disadvantaged youths. In 1968 she successfully ran for the U.S. House of Representatives, where she served until 1982.

Chisholm, like many other female legislators of the day who were not afraid to speak their minds, began her congressional career with a bang. In her first speech on the floor of the House, she attacked the war in Vietnam:

> The war in [Vietnam] was neither just nor unavoidable; it was an unnecessary war into which we stumbled, led by shortsighted, stubborn men who could not admit at any point that they were wrong but who, on the contrary, concealed their mistakes by systematically lying to the country about the nature of the war and the prospects of ending it.[5]

Shirley Chisholm (right) gets a pointer from Congresswoman Bella Abzug in 1971.

As she spoke, she made it perfectly clear that she was prepared to take action:

> We must force the administration to rethink its . . . priorities. Our children, our jobless men, our deprived, rejected, and starving fellow citizens must come first. For this reason, I intend to vote "no" on every money bill that comes to the floor of this House that provides any funds for the Department of Defense.[6]

Chisholm was labeled a troublemaker by some representatives. If she had taken such a stance during a different war, her career in the House, like Rankin's, would have been irreparably damaged. But the public's support for the war in Vietnam lessened daily as the conflict dragged on and the numbers of casualties mounted. Besides, she had at least some backing in the House and the help of Jeannette Rankin outside the chamber. Rankin, still true to her pacifist beliefs, was leading antiwar protests and encouraging her supporters to ask their representatives to bring American soldiers home.

Not only were more women of diverse backgrounds entering the House, but many, like Edith Rogers, became career politicians in the coming years. In addition to Rogers and Mink, women who have served at least eight terms in the House to date include:

Margaret Heckler	*Massachusetts*	*1967–1983*
Corrine Boggs	*Louisiana*	*1973–1991*
Patricia Schroeder	*Colorado*	*1973–1997*
Virginia Smith	*Nebraska*	*1975–1991*
Mary Rose Oakar	*Ohio*	*1977–1993*
Marge Roukema	*New Jersey*	*1981–*
Nancy Johnson	*Connecticut*	*1983–*
Marcy Kaptur	*Ohio*	*1983–*

These women have expressed a wide variety of interests and have supported many different causes. Most, though, have put children's needs, especially education, and health care at the top of their agendas.

The first woman to serve in the U.S. Senate was eighty-seven-year-old Rebecca Felton. Felton had long been involved in politics in Georgia, serving as her husband's political aide when voters sent him to Congress in 1874. When he lost a bid for reelection, Rebecca put her energy into journalism, eventually writing a weekly column for the *Atlanta Journal*. Because so many Georgians read her work, she was a well-known, highly respected personality.

In 1922, Senator Thomas Walton died, and the governor of Georgia, Thomas W. Hardwick, then had the opportunity to fill the seat with a person of his choice until an elected official could take the position. Hardwick had been deeply opposed to female suffrage, and when the amendment came up for ratification in Georgia, he made no effort to hide his disapproval. To appease the many suffragists he had antagonized and win a few of their votes in his next campaign, he decided to appoint Rebecca Felton to the vacant seat.

Even though his decision was little more than a grand gesture—she would serve for only one day—Felton gladly accepted the appointment. She used her moment in the limelight to predict the coming of female senators who would serve with distinction: "Let me say, Mr. President [the leader of the Senate], that when the women of the country come and sit with you, though there may be but a very few in the next few years, I pledge you that you will get ability, you will get integrity of purpose, you will get exalted patriotism, and you will get unstinted usefullness."[7]

Female senators were indeed on their way, albeit slowly. Nine years later, Hattie Caraway was appointed by the governor of Arkansas to complete the six-year term of her deceased husband. Caraway loved the position, so she decided to run in 1932 when her appointment ended. Her campaign was successful, making her the first woman in American history to be elected to a U.S. Senate seat. She was a staunch supporter of soldiers' and workers' rights and the Equal Rights Amendment, and served until 1945.

Ten of the next eleven female senators (Margaret Chase Smith being the exception) were appointed:

Rose Long	Louisiana	1936–1937
Dixie Graves	Alabama	1937–1938
Gladys Pyle	South Dakota	1938–1939
Vera Bushfield	South Dakota	1948
Margaret Chase Smith	Maine	1949–1973
Eva Bowring	Nebraska	1954
Hazel Able	Nebraska	1954
Maureen Neuberger	Oregon	1960–1967
Elaine Edwards	Louisiana	1972
Muriel Humphrey	Minnesota	1978
Maryon Allen	Alabama	1978

These women tended to support whatever their husbands or predecessors had, taking on few issues of their own. Although they did not bring about major changes in public policy, they altered public perception. They proved that women could be able legislators, and they conditioned the public to see them not as oddities but as forerunners.

At the same time that two senators were completing their husbands' terms in 1978, a woman finally won a seat in the Senate without first being appointed. This woman was Nancy Kassebaum. Like most earlier female legislators, Kassebaum came from a politically active family. Her father, Alf Landon, had served as governor of Kansas for two terms, and he had run, unsuccessfully, for president of the United States in 1936. Nancy shared her father's interest in politics, majoring in political science in college. She married a fellow graduate student, Philip Kassebaum, in 1956. In 1975 the Kassebaums separated, and Nancy headed to Washington to work for Senator James Pearson of Kansas. Shortly after Pearson announced that he would not run for reelection, Kassebaum decided to make a bid for his seat. Nancy's father doubted that Kansans were ready for a female senator; she proved him wrong. She not only won the election, but was reelected twice, serving until 1997.

As one of the few women in the Senate for several years (she was joined in 1981 by Floridian Paula Hawkins), Kassebaum was regarded as a spokesperson for all women. Although she was very concerned about a variety of women's issues—abortion, for example—she was also interested in foreign policy and balancing the budget, just as her male colleagues were. Her committee assignments reflected her many interests: Banking, Housing and Urban Affairs; Budget; Commerce, Science, and Transportation; Foreign Relations; and Labor and Resources, which she chaired. Her ability to serve on so many different committees whose decisions concerned all Americans, not just women or children, greatly increased the public's support for female legislators.

In 1992, Kassebaum was joined by four female senators: Dianne Feinstein and Barbara Boxer from California, who made that state the first to be represented by two women; Carol Moseley-Braun from Illinois, the first black woman to be elected to the Senate; and Patty Murray from Washington. Their political interests included gun control, early education programs, pension programs, and taxes.

In the 2000 elections, more women with more diverse backgrounds entered Congress. Hillary Rodham Clinton, for example, became the first First Lady to campaign for and win a Senate seat, bringing a unique voice to that chamber.

From First Lady to New York State senator, Hillary Rodham Clinton celebrates her 2000 victory with her daughter, Chelsea, and her husband, outgoing president Bill Clinton.

Only four women have served in both the House and Senate—Margaret Chase Smith, Olympia Snowe, Barbara Mikulski, and Barbara Boxer. As most female legislators did in the early days, Margaret Chase Smith entered politics on her husband's coattails. When he died in 1940, she was appointed to his seat in the House. After her appointment expired, she successfully campaigned for the position, serving as a representative from Maine until 1949. Smith was quite a contrast to Jeannette Rankin, vocally supporting America's entry into World War II. In 1949, Smith ran—again, successfully—for the Senate, where she was the only woman for twenty-five years.

Although Margaret Chase Smith fought for many issues, she is best remembered for two things: courage and roses. In 1950, Smith boldly stood up to Senator Joseph McCarthy, who used the free-speech protection provided in the Senate to accuse anyone who disagreed with him of being a Communist. At the time, many Americans believed that Communist nations, especially the Soviet Union, were run by powerful dictators who employed thousands of spies who devised plots to infiltrate democracies to make them ripe for a takeover. As a result, to be called a "commie" was a serious verbal attack that could ruin one's life. Smith argued that it was time to stop the character assassination. In the process, she put her political career at risk. But shortly after, a few senators, inspired by Smith's courage, decided to stand up to McCarthy, setting the scene in the Senate for his eventual downfall.

In 1964, Smith was one of the presidential nominees at the Republican National Convention. She was the first woman to have her name placed in nomination by a major political party.

Smith, who held a Senate seat until 1973, almost always wore a rose on her lapel. In 1987, President Ronald Reagan signed into law a bill that made the rose the official flower of the United States in her honor.

Another woman from Maine who has served in both the House (1973, 1979–1994) and the Senate (1994–) is Olympia Snowe. Snowe completed her husband's term when he died in 1973. In 1979 she ran for the House on her own. Her interests in Congress have included better health care for the aged, energy conservation programs, more funding for day care for young children, and the end of discrimination in pension laws, which would benefit women.

One of Snowe's colleagues in the House was Barbara Mikulski, a former social worker. Mikulski, the daughter of Polish immigrants, had no family connections to help her win or train her for a congressional office. Instead, she ran on her own after becoming involved in local politics in Maryland. She served in the House from 1977 to 1987, when she successfully ran for the Senate. In both chambers, she was regarded as a "brawler," who readily fought for what she believed. Mikulski's special interests have included health care, strict guidelines for disposal of hazardous waste, and ending discrimination in the workplace.

Barbara Boxer is known as a strong advocate for women's rights. Her agenda is fueled by the discrimination she faced as a young woman. When she finished college and applied for a job as a stockbroker, she was told that women couldn't be brokers. Later, while unsuccessfully running for political office in Marin County, California, in 1971, voters told her to abandon her political dreams and go home and take care of her husband and children. But Boxer refused to give up her political aspirations, and she ran again four years later. This time she won.

In 1982 she ran for the House, where she served for ten years. While there, she fought for spending restraints in the military, and she wrote the Violence Against Women Act, which funded rape-prevention programs and shelters for victims of domestic abuse.

In 1992, Boxer was elected to the Senate. Her agenda included gun control, education, health, and environmental issues.

Yet at the same time, an old custom continued. Jean Carnahan, First Lady of Missouri, was appointed to the Senate when Missourians voted for her deceased husband. Governor Mel Carnahan had been campaigning for the Senate when he died in a plane crash on October 16, less than a month before voters were to go to the polls. It was too late to remove Mel Carnahan's name from the ballot, so Jean Carnahan agreed to go to Washington to carry out her husband's political plans if Missourians voted for him—they did, in large numbers—until a special election could be held.

The 2000 elections made history in other ways as well. Women won 16 percent of all congressional seats. This contrasted sharply with the number of successful female candidates in 1977, which had once been considered a banner year. In that election, women won 4 percent of all positions in Congress. The 2000 results, though, were not representative of America, for women accounted for approximately half the population. This caused some women to complain about "taxation without representation," a phrase that goes all the way back to the Revolutionary War. Still, Penelope Barker, Jeannette Rankin, and Rebecca Felton would have been proud of the progress that female legislators had made.

CHAPTER 5

On the Local Scene

The opportunity to give back to the community, to solve problems by creating solutions and knowing what you do today will reap benefits for your children and grandchildren, has its own rewards that can be articulated in any language.
— Rita Mullins, mayor of Palatine, Illinois, 1989–

While some women were dreaming about going to Washington, D.C., to fight for issues that affected their lives and the lives of their friends, neighbors, and loved ones, others turned to their states and communities for similar opportunities. These women wanted to make a difference, too, and they quickly learned that there were literally thousands of opportunities to do so.

States have three levels of government: state; county or borough (in Louisiana's case, parish); and municipal (city, town, or village). State governments are structured like our federal government; they have legislative, executive, and judicial branches. In each state, voters elect legislators who then pass laws that have statewide impact. These wide-ranging laws determine, among many other things, the length of the school year; the amount of money citizens pay for state taxes; how taxes are spent; what regulations—if any—should be placed on local businesses; what constitutes an illegal act; and how the state's environment is to be protected. Voters also elect executives to carry out these laws, usually a governor, lieutenant governor, secretary of state, attorney general, and treasurer. Many judges are elected as well. They supervise trials and interpret state laws.

Counties are run by boards that are often called "agents of the state" because they carry out its laws. Elected board members and the board's elected leader decide how best to proceed, and then give directions to other officials, often chosen by voters. These officials, depending on which position they won, collect taxes, record vital information required by the state (birth, death, marriage, and property records), supervise elections, maintain county roads, arrest anyone accused of breaking state laws, and try the accused on behalf of the state. County board members also pass local regulations called ordinances. Some counties have their own parks, hiking trails, and health facilities; if so, elected officials are responsible for their oversight as well.

City, village, and town boards (or councils) and their elected or appointed leaders deal with local problems and services. These boards maintain city streets and town roads; establish fire and police departments; determine zoning and building regulations, which may require the approval of county boards; and, if members want to get elected again, make sure that the garbage is picked up on schedule. Like county board members, municipal officials can pass ordinances.

Although the number of elected positions varies from state to state and from time to time, most states, counties, and municipalities offer many opportunities for would-be politicians. Wisconsin, for example, a medium-sized state, has 132 state legislators and 6 state executives. It also has 72 counties, 189 cities, 395 villages, 1,266 towns, and 426 school districts, all of which are run by elected officials.

Even though many female politicians have held state and local offices throughout the United States, as always, certain firsts stand out. The first female state governors, Nellie Tayloe Ross of Wyoming, and Miriam Amanda Ferguson of Texas, began their gubernatorial careers in 1925. Because Ross took her oath on January 5, fifteen days before Ferguson did, Ross is considered America's first woman governor.

Like many female politicians in high places, Ross followed her husband, Governor William Ross, who died on October 2, 1924, into office. Wyoming law stated that a special election had to be held, and Nellie Ross, after numerous consultations with Democratic party officials, reluctantly agreed to run for her husband's former position. She was not comfortable in the spotlight, and she did

Governor Nellie Tayloe Ross of Wyoming poses with the ceremonial first shovelful of dirt from the construction of airplane hangars in Cheyenne in 1925.

little campaigning on the issues. Instead, she told voters that casting a ballot for her was a tribute to her husband's memory as well as an affirmation of William Ross's plans for the state, which she vowed to fulfill.

Nellie Ross's election generated lots of publicity. Shortly after, she became the focus of curiosity seekers, and it was not unusual for her to find people sitting on her porch or parading past her office so that they could get a glimpse of her.

Ross eventually ran into trouble with Wyoming's Republican-controlled legislature. Voters sided with the lawmakers, especially on tax issues, so Ross, whom historians consider an able administrator, became a one-term governor.

In contrast, Miriam Amanda "Ma" Ferguson, who received considerably lower grades for her ability to govern from historians,

Governor Miriam Amanda "Ma" Ferguson (far left in first row) at an event in Texas during one of her terms in office. "Pa" Ferguson, as named in the picture's caption, stands fifth from left.

served two terms, 1925–1927 and 1933–1935. Like Ross, she, too, followed her husband into office, but under vastly different circumstances. When James Ferguson was convicted on seven counts of misappropriation of public funds during his second term in office and by state law could not run for a political position, his wife ran in his place.

Ferguson's first term was plagued with controversy. Instead of misuse of funds, though, she was accused of being a bit too free with pardons and paroles, issuing, on average, a hundred per month. She was also accused of granting the best road contracts to her husband's friends in exchange for land or cash, sometimes both. Angry legislators started impeachment proceedings, hoping to remove her from office before her term expired. The drive failed. However, it had a temporary impact on voters; when Ferguson ran in 1926 for the governorship, she was defeated.

But the Fergusons weren't willing to leave the political scene. Arguing that they needed a chance to clear their names, James Ferguson decided to run for governor again in 1930. He appealed to the courts to have his name placed on the ballot, a plea that was denied. So Miriam Ferguson ran, unsuccessfully, in his place. Still unwilling to give up, and campaigning against corruption in government—a charge that raised more than a few eyebrows—she won reelection in 1932.

Another woman who followed her husband into office was Lurleen Wallace; she ran for the governorship of Alabama in 1967, when her husband, Governor George Wallace, wasn't allowed, by law, to run for a third consecutive term. George Wallace did most of the campaigning, promising voters that they would get two governors if they elected his wife. Lurleen Wallace became seriously ill shortly after taking her oath, and she died in office.

While many of the first women in office gained entry through their husbands, those who followed sought positions in their own right. This was often a slow process, for it took a lot of time to duplicate the experience that male politicians already had. To begin their own political careers, would-be female politicians volunteered their time, serving as mentors in schools and then running for school boards or working on civic committees before campaigning for the city council. Others joined political parties to gain support from party regulars while learning how to run a campaign.

One of these self-made women was Ella Grasso, the first woman to serve as governor (Connecticut, 1975–1981) in her own right. Grasso became interested in politics in the early 1940s. She was an active member of the League of Women Voters and a volunteer for the Democratic party before running for office. After serving two terms in her state's legislature, Grasso ran for secretary of state in Connecticut in 1958, a post she won and held for twelve years. In 1970, citing her political experience, she successfully ran for the U.S. House of Representatives. She was reelected in 1972.

In 1974, Grasso turned her attention back to state politics, announcing, with great optimism, her candidacy for governor of Connecticut. This decision did not sit well with the leaders of the state's Democratic party, who openly doubted that a woman could win. Grasso ignored them. "The judgment will be made of me as an individual," she said, "on the basis of what I have accomplished in my career in public life. . . .Four years ago, I might have had some difficulty in advancing a viable candidacy as a woman, but it's a non-issue now."[1] She handily defeated other Democratic hopefuls in the primaries, forcing party leaders to endorse her.

Grasso's first term was a difficult one, since Connecticut was deeply in debt. Governor Grasso had to use all her political skills to persuade different interests in the state to come together to solve the state's serious economic problems, which meant cutting costs and persuading the public that a sales tax was necessary if the debt was to be paid. She was very successful in her endeavors, and when she ran for reelection, she had little to fear from her opponents.

In the coming years, she was followed by other female governors:

Dixie Lee Ray	*Washington*	*1977–1981*
Martha Layne Collins	*Kentucky*	*1984–1987*
Madeleine Kunin	*Vermont*	*1985–1991*
Kay Orr	*Nebraska*	*1987–1991*
Rose Mofford	*Arizona*	*1988–1991*

Ann Richards	Texas	1991–1995
Barbara Roberts	Oregon	1991–1995
Joan Finney	Kansas	1991–1995
Christine Todd Whitman	New Jersey	1994–2001
Jeanne Shaheen	New Hampshire	1997–
Jane Dee Hull	Arizona	1997–
Judy Martz	Montana	2001–
Ruth Minner	Delaware	2001–
Jane Swift	Massachusetts	2001–2002

Nancy Hollister also served as a governor, although very briefly. As lieutenant governor of Ohio, she assumed the governorship, taking office when the governor resigned to become a legislator in Washington in late 1998. She resigned a few weeks later to do likewise.

Besides being elected to the governor's office, female politicians have also served in other state executive positions. Although their numbers grew slowly over the years, in 2000, women held 28 percent of the more than three hundred offices available. In addition, for the first time, women completely dominated an executive branch in a state. In Arizona, voters selected women to be the governor, secretary of state, attorney general, treasurer, and superintendent of public instruction.

Women have also made significant gains as state legislators. In 1924, eighty-four women served in state senates or assemblies. Five years later, two hundred women did so. While this was a significant increase, fewer than 1 percent of state lawmakers were female in 1929. In 2001, however, women held 23 percent of these positions.

Not only are women winning more of these positions, some have become leaders in their state senates and houses. In 1999, New Hampshire, which had a female governor at the time, made history when Beverly Hollingworth was elected by her colleagues to lead the state senate, the first female in New Hampshire to hold such a position. Hollingworth's counterpart in the house, Donna Sytek, was the first woman to lead New Hampshire's other chamber. Together, they were the first female pair to lead a state legislature.

Even so, Sytek did not consider this event unusual or unpredictable. She pointed out that women had been elected to the state legislature since 1970. "It was only a matter of time until we'd have presiding officers," she said. Nor did she think that being female affected her campaign for the position. "I don't think gender has anything to do with it. It's more a matter of your approach to the Legislature."[2]

∽

Among the most famous events in municipality history were the elections of the first all-female town councils, which took place in Jackson Hole, Wyoming, and Yoncalla, Oregon, in 1920. To achieve these results, women voted in large numbers, and in the Yoncalla election, the town's women also devised a clever scheme to guarantee victory. They believed that local officials, all of whom were running for reelection, had done little or nothing to solve the town's problems. So the women, rather than choose among the men on the ballot, secretly pledged to write in the names of female candidates who had agreed to hold office. When the ballots were examined and counted, according to an account of the day, the

The all-female town council of Yoncalla, Oregon, in 1920, with Mayor Mary Burt in the center

women "had risen in their wrath . . . and swept every masculine office-holder out of his job."[3] The men had little to say but that they were "much surprised."

History is full of stories about women who led small communities in the 1920s. However, it was the first female mayor of a large city, Bertha Knight Landes, who made national headlines when she became the leader of Seattle, Washington, in 1926. Landes had served on the city council for four years before running for mayor. Upset by the crime she saw all around her, she told voters that it was time to do some "municipal housecleaning." She vowed, "If elected mayor I promise to wage a relentless warfare on all crooks, thieves, bandits, burglars, stick-up men and other law-defying characters."[4]

After receiving 80 percent of the vote, close to 100 percent from local women's organizations, Landes set out to fulfill her pledge with a vengeance, targeting those in power who had allowed crime to flourish. This included firing William Severyns, Seattle's chief of police, who openly bragged about corruption in the police force, and Roy Olmstead, a lieutenant in the police department who routinely smuggled rum from Canada into Seattle. At the time, manufacturing and selling alcohol was illegal in the United States.

Landes was only one of a long line of women who headed their communities. Some, such as Dianne Feinstein (San Francisco), who later became a U.S. senator, Kathy Whitmire (Houston), and Jane Byrne (Chicago), because of the enormous problems they faced, became well-known national figures. Their successes created more opportunities for women to lead. In 2000, 20 percent of all mayors of large American cities (30,000 or more people) were women. Political pros have predicted that this number, like the number of female state executives, state legislators, and county board officials, will continue to grow in the future.

CHAPTER 6

In the Courtroom

Justice is better than chivalry if we cannot have both.
—Alice Stone Blackwell, suffragist

Courtroom scenes in the movies are full of drama. Smug prosecutors present overwhelming evidence to a gullible jury and dour judge, while idealistic defense lawyers struggle against all odds to save the life of an innocent client. Meanwhile, overeager reporters hover in the background, waiting for a decision that is destined to make national headlines.

Although such scenes are not unheard of in real life, American courtrooms are more often the sites of less riveting, though no less important, events. Every day trials of all kinds are held in lower courts on the state and federal levels. At the same time, appeals courts, usually headed by a panel of three judges, again on both state and federal levels, rule on previous trials, deciding whether the accused had a fair hearing. The results of these cases seldom make more than the local evening news, if that.

However, events in state supreme courts and the U.S. Supreme Court, whose duty it is to interpret laws and strike down legislation that is unconstitutional, almost always attract a lot of attention. Part of the reason is that decisions made here have long-term, far-reaching effects. *Brown* v. *Board of Education of Topeka, Kansas*, a U.S. Supreme Court decision in 1954, is a good example. Still the law of the land almost fifty years later, this case made it illegal for all American school boards, not just the board of education in Topeka, Kansas, where the case was first heard, to practice segregation. Until then, many black children were not allowed to sit in classrooms with their white counterparts. Instead, blacks were forced to attend separate schools that were usually poorly equipped and understaffed. The Court ruled that segregation did irreparable harm to blacks, because it taught them to regard themselves as second-class citizens. Since the Fourteenth Amendment prohibited states from treating its citizens differently, segregation, the Court said, had to stop. This decision reversed a judgment made by the Court in 1896 that permitted separate facilities.

Since our laws are open to interpretation and court decisions are so important to all Americans, most citizens want judges who share their values and beliefs. Voters can help determine who sits on the bench as judge, for even though our judicial system is supposed to be above the fray of politics, it is not. In general, judges serving in state courts run for their position. In the case of federal courts, the president of the United States makes the selections, which then have to be approved by the Senate. To distance judges from voters and remove political influences once the men and women are in office, state judges, especially those on supreme courts, often serve for long periods of time. Federal judges are appointed for life.

Because so much is at stake, struggles over who will serve on the bench are not uncommon, and sometimes these struggles have become downright cantankerous. A perfect example is the battle that took place over a U.S. Supreme Court position in 1991. When Justice Thurgood Marshall retired that year, President George Bush nominated Clarence Thomas to the Court. Bush was under great pressure to choose both a black and a conservative (in general, one who does not want the government to play a large role in the lives of its citizens), and the president publicly argued that Thomas was the best possible choice. Not everyone agreed.

After being nominated, would-be justices are questioned by the Senate Judiciary Committee. If the committee approves the nominee, he or she is then presented to the full Senate for confirmation. In 1991 the committee, consisting of fourteen white men, was deeply divided; half were conservative, half were the opposite, or liberal. In addition, all were well aware that the nine-member Court was also divided. If Thomas joined the bench, the liberals said, the Court could become conservative, a possibility that made them very nervous. Trying to determine just how conservative Thomas was, the liberals grilled him at length on one of the most hotly contested issues of the day: affirmative action. This program gave women and minorities, who had been discriminated against in the past, an edge in schooling and employment opportunities. Because it was so controversial, it was likely to be challenged in the Court in the near future. When Thomas made it clear that he opposed affirmative action, those who supported it rushed to Washington to testify against him.

In addition, Anita Hill, a law professor at the University of Oklahoma, went to the capital with yet another concern: sexual harassment. She told the committee—actually, the whole nation, for the hearings raised so much interest they were televised—that Clarence Thomas, with whom she had worked in the past, had made inappropriate comments to her that had poisoned her working environment. He was not, she argued, a good choice for the Court. Thomas vehemently denied Hill's charges. But women who thought Hill's accusations had the ring of truth to them became incensed by the alleged comments as well as some of the committee members' failure to take the sexual harassment issue seriously. In the end, following a lot of verbal wrangling, Thomas's nomination was passed on to the Senate by a seven-to-seven vote.

After extensive lobbying on the part of blacks who favored affirmative action and women who understood the humiliation of sexual harassment, Thomas's nomination came up for a vote. Although opponents continued to argue that there were simply too many questions surrounding this nominee, Thomas was confirmed, fifty-two to forty-eight.

Deeply alarmed by the outcome and wanting greater influence in the future, women in the Senate vowed to fight for positions on the Judiciary Committee. They also encouraged other women to run for the Senate. Barbara Boxer, who successfully ran for the chamber from California in 1992, credited the Thomas hearings as helping her make up her mind to campaign for a Senate seat. She wanted to be able to vote on the next Court nominee.

When women first turned their attention to the courtroom in the 1800s, they did so as lawyers, a professional accomplishment that was difficult to achieve. Few law schools would accept female students then; professors worried that having women in classrooms would be distracting to male students. Also, some states actually forbade women from becoming attorneys. When this rule was challenged in 1873, the Supreme Court ruled in *Bradwell* v. *Illinois* that it was legal for states to keep women out of the profession if they wished to do so. After all, the Court said, "The paramount destiny and mission of [women] are to fulfill the noble and benign offices of wife and mother. This is the law of the Creator."[1] As if these hurdles weren't enough, even if states permitted women to become attorneys, there was the question of whether a state bar association would accredit a woman, and without a bar's blessings, a lawyer couldn't present a case in court.

The first woman to be admitted to the legal profession was Arabella Mansfield. In 1869 the Iowa bar granted her permission to argue in state courts after she convinced members that her intensive studies—on her own—were equal to a law-school education. The women who followed her had to find sympathetic males who would fight for women's admittance to law schools, overturn legislation that said a woman couldn't be a lawyer, and present candidates to bar associations for approval. With such help, women slowly made inroads into the profession. By 2000, 44 percent of all law students and 24 percent of all attorneys were female. In 2001, for the first time in American history, the majority of law students were women.

One of the important aspects of having female lawyers in the judicial system is their empathy for—and their willingness to take on—causes that have special significance to women. One such cause is abortion. Until 1973, abortion was illegal in the United States unless it could be proved that the life of the mother was in danger. This doesn't mean that abortions didn't take place. Women turned to back-alley clinics where, because the risk of infection and complications was high, many died.

When a young woman in Texas, Norma McCorvey, known historically as Jane Roe, became pregnant, she appealed for help. Uneducated and barely able to support herself, she wanted an abortion. Supporters passed her name on to Sarah Weddington, a lawyer and a former member of the state legislature who had long before volunteered to test Texas's antiabortion laws in court. Henry Wade, the district attorney in Dallas, defended the laws.

This case, known as *Roe* v. *Wade*, eventually reached the Supreme Court. When the Court decided that an abortion was a private matter and that the justice system had no right to interfere, some Americans were deeply upset. Believing that a different Court might reverse this decision, these Americans pleaded, prayed, and pushed for justices who would overturn *Roe* v. *Wade*.

Sarah Weddington was but one of many attorneys who argued for women's rights before the Court. Few, however, have made as impressive a list of accomplishments as Ruth Bader Ginsburg. Ginsburg, who studied at Harvard, then Columbia Law School, tied for first in her class when she received her degree in 1959. But despite her outstanding credentials, she could not find a law firm that would hire her. "A woman, a Jew, and a mother. Three strikes. It was too much," she said years later when explaining why so many firms turned her down.[2] Although Ginsburg finally found a job clerking for a federal judge, in 1961 she decided to accept an offer at Rutgers University in New Jersey, where she became a professor of law.

At the same time, Ginsburg also agreed to take on some cases for the American Civil Liberties Union (ACLU). By 1960, almost 38 percent of women worked outside the home. Many were paid less money than men even if they were performing the same tasks. Working women were also denied access to some jobs simply because they were female. In addition, many companies thought wives belonged at home, and some firms would not hire them. Just as upsetting, wives could not establish credit in their own names— even if they did manage to find a full-time job. Angry and frustrated, women turned to the courts for help. When it became apparent that many cases were in the offing, the ACLU set up the Women's Rights Project and asked Ginsburg to head it.

Ginsburg developed a plan of action that was simple and successful. She chose her cases carefully, picking those that clearly violated the equal-protection clause of the Fourteenth Amendment. For example, the first case she argued before the U.S. Supreme Court was *Frontiero v. Richardson*. Lieutenant Sharon Frontiero, an Air Force physical therapist, was denied health benefits for her husband that were routinely made available to her male peers who had wives. "Two people in the military, both the same rank, one gets more than the other," Ginsburg told the Court.[3] How could that be fair? she wondered. On May 14, 1973, the Court issued its decision. It ordered all the armed services, not just the Air Force, to grant all personnel of equal rank equal pay and equal benefits.

Ginsburg then used this decision as a precedent, quoting the justices' words when fighting the next case, and when that was won, using the Court's statements from the two previous cases, and so on. From 1973 to 1976, Ginsburg presented six gender discrimination cases to the Court; she won five.

⛏

As soon as women had a toehold in the legal profession, they began to eye positions as judges. Once again, there were some impressive firsts: Florence Ellinwood Allen, Constance Baker Motley, and Sandra Day O'Connor.

Florence Ellinwood Allen was one of the first women to serve on a state court as well as the first to serve on a federal bench. The daughter of pioneers in the Utah Territory who could trace her ancestry back to Revolutionary War hero Ethan Allen, Florence Ellinwood Allen attended school in Ohio, while her father served as the Territory's first representative in the House. In 1914 she was accepted by the Ohio Bar Association, which gave her the right to present cases in state courtrooms. Nevertheless, she was unable to find a job. Allen then decided to open her own office. She also routinely volunteered her services to local suffrage groups and became an active member of the local Democratic party, in the process gaining valuable political know-how that would serve her well in the years to come.

In 1919, Allen used her political knowledge to lobby for an appointment. Within months, she became an assistant prosecutor of Cuyahoga County.

Once the Nineteenth Amendment was passed, Allen announced that she was running for Ohio's Court of Common Pleas. Suffragists carried her petitions—she needed thousands of signatures to get on the ballot—and Allen gave speeches to anyone who would listen. She defeated nine candidates for the post.

Judge Allen refused to have her trials limited to divorce and domestic abuse cases, which other judges thought she should take simply because she was a woman. Aware that she was breaking ground and eager to have other women follow her as full-fledged professionals, she insisted on hearing a variety of cases. She was, she said, a real judge who could handle any type of trial. Also, she insisted that women be included in juries, believing that they brought a different perspective to deliberations. How could a female defendant really have a fair trial, she argued, if she wasn't judged by at least a few of her true peers—other women?

In 1922, after presiding over more than eight hundred hearings in two years, Allen used her experience to successfully run for the Ohio Supreme Court. The state's women were so taken with the idea that a female could actually sit on Ohio's highest bench, they formed sixty-six Florence Allen clubs across the state to help her win.

In 1934, President Franklin D. Roosevelt, deeply impressed by Allen's accomplishments and eager to end a male monopoly in the federal court system, nominated Judge Allen for a position on the U.S. Sixth Circuit Court of Appeals. Although she was unanimously confirmed by the Senate, not all her fellow judges were thrilled with her appointment. Rather than sit on the bench with her, one judge called in sick several days in a row. When he realized his "illness" had little effect on Allen, he made a rapid recovery and returned to work.

Well aware that lots of eyes were on her again, Allen set high standards for herself, which she believed paid off royally. "Judges who were at first opposed to women officials," she said later, "accepted us when we handled our work steadily and conscientiously."[4] She served on this court for twenty-five years, the last few years as the chief judge.

The next female judge to make history was Constance Baker Motley. Motley had more than twenty years of legal experience behind her before being appointed to a court. She received her law degree from Columbia University in 1946. With her husband's encouragement, she joined a local chapter of the National Association for the Advancement of Colored People (NAACP) when, simply because she was black, she was denied access to a local beach. (Segregation affected more than schools. Many public facilities were off-limits to blacks until the late 1960s.) Shortly after, she joined the NAACP's Legal Defense and Educational Fund team in New York. Motley worked on high-profile civil-rights cases, including *Brown* v. *Board of Education*, personally arguing ten civil-rights cases before the U.S. Supreme Court. She won nine of them.

President Lyndon B. Johnson was deeply committed to the Civil Rights Movement. When an opening occurred in the federal courts, he sought out experienced judges from minority groups to fill these vacancies. In 1966 he appointed Constance Baker Motley to the federal bench.

Although no one verbally objected to her nomination at her hearing, Motley, like Judge Allen, still faced opposition. Senator James Eastland, a segregationist and chairman of the committee, refused to attend the hearing, knowing full well that he couldn't stop the committee from approving Johnson's choice. Instead, he counted on raising a ruckus in the Senate. First, he delayed Motley's confirmation hearings for almost seven months, a tactic President Johnson challenged by refusing to nominate anyone else for any judgeship—even if seats in the federal courts would be vacant—until Motley had had her day in the Senate. Rather than attacking her for her race or sex, Eastland accused her of being a Communist. His mean-spirited tactics failed, though, and Motley became the first black woman to become a federal judge.

Like Allen, Motley set high standards, making it possible for more women to become judges. When she took her position in 1966, she was one of four females on the federal bench. These women accounted for less than 1 percent of all federal judgeships. Twenty years later, women held 7 percent of all seats in federal courts. This growth plus the fact that women were studying law in increasing numbers surprised Judge Motley. "I never thought I would live long enough to see the legal profession change to the extent it has," she said upon her retirement in 1986. "It's a new day."[5] Twelve years later, women held 19 percent of all federal judgeships.

Even more striking was the fact that when Judge Motley retired, a woman was a U.S. Supreme Court Justice, an accomplishment that had been unthinkable when Motley began to practice law. On September 25, 1981, President Ronald Reagan swore in Sandra Day O'Connor as the 102nd person and the first woman to sit on the nation's highest court.

O'Connor was an outstanding choice. She held a law degree from one of the nation's most prestigious schools, Stanford, where she had graduated third in her class in 1952. One of the two men before her in class rank was William Rehnquist, with whom she would serve on the bench twenty-nine years later. But despite her high grades, the only job offer O'Connor received after graduation was for a position as a legal secretary.

In 1956, O'Connor and her husband moved to Arizona, where they both were accredited by the Arizona Bar Association and where she began her political career. Sandra Day O'Connor practiced law until her second child was born, at which time she became an active volunteer in her community and in the local branch of the Republican party. In 1966 one of Arizona's senators in the state legislature resigned, and the governor appointed O'Connor to take his place. Her work was so highly respected—she was especially good at

Sandra Day O'Connor was sworn in as a Supreme Court justice by Chief Justice Warren Burger (left) on September 25, 1981. O'Connor's husband, John, holds the family Bible.

drafting legislation—that voters returned her to office several times. In 1972 her colleagues selected her to be the senate majority leader. While in the state senate, O'Connor supported the Equal Rights Amendment. She also fought for fairer property laws for Arizona's wives; until the 1970s, all property owned by a husband and wife was under the control of the husband.

In 1974, O'Connor turned her attention to the courtroom. She campaigned for and won a position on the Maricopa County Superior Court. Her work there caught the eye of Governor Bruce Babbitt, who, one year later, nominated O'Connor for the Arizona Court of Appeals. When an opening occurred on the U.S. Supreme Court, President Reagan, persuaded by Arizona's senators that they knew the perfect candidate, nominated O'Connor. The Senate vote to confirm her was 99 to 0.

O'Connor's appointment was hailed with joy, and she received more than four thousand letters of congratulations, the vast majority of them from women. "It's been touching," Justice O'Connor said, "to see how women of all ages have responded to the appointment of a woman to the Court."[6]

O'Connor has been one of the Court's most interesting justices. Sometimes her votes seemed conservative and at other times liberal, keeping political pros guessing. The only issue that she has never wavered on is women's rights. She has consistently voted to strike down laws that promoted discrimination based on gender.

In 1993, O'Connor was joined on the Supreme Court by Ruth Bader Ginsburg, who, after making history in her fight to end sex discrimination, had served as a federal district judge from 1980 to 1993. Ginsburg's appointment brought the percentage of women on the highest court to 22.

The number of women serving on state supreme courts has also increased. In 2001, women held 20 percent of all available positions on these courts, and forty-nine of the fifty states—South Dakota being the exception—have had at least one female state supreme court justice in their history. Also, female justices have served in the majority on state supreme courts in Michigan and Minnesota. In short, by the twenty-first century, women's presence was certainly felt in the courtroom—a real change from Susan B. Anthony's day, when she wasn't even allowed to testify on her own behalf.

CHAPTER 7

Presidential Advisers

I know what's best for the President. I put him in the White House.

——Florence Harding, First Lady 1921–1923

To date, no woman has served as president of the United States. But this doesn't mean that women haven't had at least some influence in the executive office. Many First Ladies, for example, have served as one of their husbands' political advisers. They have suggested campaign issues and strategies before elections and given advice afterward.

Mary Todd Lincoln is a good example of a politically ambitious wife. She insisted on choosing the pictures that were used on Abraham Lincoln's campaign posters. She also listened to him debate his opponent, Stephen A. Douglas, after which she critiqued her husband's arguments. In addition, Mary Lincoln contacted leaders in her husband's political party to seek campaign advice, then encouraged her husband to make use of the best suggestions. After the election, Mary Lincoln repeatedly voiced her opinion about the advisers he chose. "My husband," she once said, "placed great confidence in my knowledge of human nature."[1]

Eleanor Roosevelt also played an important part in her husband's career, serving as Franklin D. Roosevelt's substitute when he was struck down by polio and could no longer give numerous speeches or attend political meetings. After his election, she encouraged him to fill at least some vacancies in the executive branch with women.

To bolster confidence during the Great Depression (1929–1936) and World War II, two crises during which her husband was presi-

Franklin D. and Eleanor Roosevelt on the campaign trail in 1932

dent, Eleanor Roosevelt spent her days among the people, listening to their concerns. She visited workers trying to find jobs and wounded soldiers in hospitals, then reported her experiences to her husband. Even if she had no answers, Americans believed that someone was really listening to them. This made their burden a little lighter.

Another example of a politically active First Lady was Hillary Rodham Clinton. Not only did she advise her husband, Bill Clinton, during his presidential campaigns, she fought for causes in which they both believed after his election. One of these was changing America's health-care system, which had become very complex and expensive. After months of study, Hillary Clinton presented a proposal to Congress. Even though it was not accepted, the very fact that a First Lady could approach Congress indicated how powerful a president's wife could be. It is for this very reason that Americans scrutinize a candidate's spouse very carefully during a campaign.

Besides being influenced by their wives, presidents have also been swayed by their cabinet officers, some of whom have been women. George Washington had the fewest officers: a secretary of state, a secretary of the treasury, a secretary of war, and an attorney general. All were men, since women were neither encouraged to participate in running the government then nor had the education or background to do so. By the late 1900s, the number of cabinet officers had risen to fourteen, and both genders were represented. Besides the four members Washington had, presidents were advised by secretaries of the departments of the interior, agriculture, commerce, labor, health and human services, housing and urban development, transportation, energy, education, and veterans affairs. Also, the secretary of war was now known as the secretary of defense.

Each president chooses his officers, who appear before special Senate committees for questioning. If a committee accepts the president's nominee, he or she is presented to the Senate for confirmation, where the would-be officer must receive a vote of confidence from two-thirds of the members.

Cabinet officers serve as long as their performance pleases the president—that is, as long as they eagerly spearhead the president's projects, run their departments efficiently, and avoid unfavorable publicity. Cabinet members also give advice when asked to do so, although the president is at no time required to take it. Once when President Lincoln's entire cabinet opposed him on an issue, Lincoln announced, "Seven nays and one aye. The ayes have it."[2]

The first woman to serve in a president's cabinet was Secretary of Labor Frances Perkins, who was a member during Franklin D. Roosevelt's four terms in office (1933–1945). Perkins had an impressive background in labor relations. Trained as a social worker, she was deeply involved in reform efforts aimed at improving working conditions for laborers in New York City. In the

As the first woman to serve as secretary of labor, Frances Perkins sometimes had to deal with skeptical male workers. Here she greets workers at a Carnegie Steel plant in Pittsburgh, Pennsylvania.

early 1900s, it was not unusual for men to toil ten hours a day, six days a week for as little as $15. For the same number of hours, women seldom earned more than $6. In addition, many factories were poorly heated and ventilated, and some were little more than firetraps. This was especially true in the garment industry, where fabric scraps were piled next to oily rags used to clean the sewing machines, and a spark could set a factory ablaze.

After Perkins witnessed the burning to death of 146 workers in the Triangle Shirtwaist Company fire in New York City in 1911, she set out to make sure that such a tragedy never happened again. She went to work for the Committee on Safety of the City of New York. She also made recommendations to the State Factory Investigating Committee. As she traveled about, she cited one example after another of dangerous working conditions. The state legislature reacted by passing bills that forced manufacturers to provide better working conditions.

Because of her highly visible position and her willingness to speak out, Perkins attracted a lot of attention. Therefore, when Franklin Roosevelt became president, many women, including Eleanor Roosevelt, suggested that Perkins become secretary of labor.

As secretary, Frances Perkins led a national crusade to better workers' lives. She fought for laws that set a minimum wage and a maximum number of hours men and women could be expected to work. She also strengthened the women's and children's bureaus, giving them more power to enforce labor laws that protected these two groups from exploitation. In addition, she improved the federal mediation service so it could better resolve differences between workers and employers, and she laid the groundwork for the Social Security Act, which provided a financial safety net for all workers.

Although Perkins proved that a woman could be a very effective secretary of labor, the next woman to hold her position, Ann Dore McLaughlin, didn't join a presidential cabinet until 1987. She served two years. McLaughlin was followed by Elizabeth Dole (1989–1990), a former secretary of transportation (1983–1987); Lynn Martin (1991–1993), who had served in the House for ten years; Alexis Herman (1997–2001), a former director of the Women's Bureau in the Labor Department; and Elaine Chao (2001–), a former director of the Peace Corps.

Another trailblazer and the second woman to hold a cabinet position was Oveta Culp Hobby. She became the secretary of health, education, and welfare in 1953. Hobby had served as the director of the Women's Auxiliary Army Corps during World War II, the first-of-its-kind program for which Representative Edith Nourse Rogers had fought. Hobby's leadership during the war attracted the attention of General Dwight Eisenhower, and when he became president, he chose Hobby to be a cabinet member. As secretary, Hobby led a national drive for hospital construction and a massive distribution program of the Salk polio vaccine, especially for children. She resigned in 1955 to care for her seriously ill husband.

To date, only three women have held Hobby's position. In 1979, Patricia Harris, the first black woman to join a president's cabinet and a former dean of Howard University's Law School, became the secretary of what was now known as the Department of Health and Human Services; by this time, education had become a department of its own. Harris had previously served as the secretary of housing and urban development in 1977. She was secretary of health and human services until 1981. Margaret Heckler, who had served in the House for sixteen years, was the secretary from 1983 until 1985. Donna E. Shalala, a former chancellor of the University of Wisconsin, took the position ten years later. She was secretary until 2001.

In addition, nine other women have been cabinet members:

Carla Hills	secretary of housing and urban development	1975–1977
Juanita Kreps	secretary of commerce	1977–1979
Shirley M. Hufstedler	secretary of education	1979–1981
Barbara H. Franklin	secretary of commerce	1992–1993
Hazel O'Leary	secretary of energy	1993–1997
Janet Reno	attorney general	1993–2001
Madeleine Albright	secretary of state	1996–2001
Gale Norton	secretary of the interior	2001–
Ann Veneman	secretary of agriculture	2001–

When Madeleine Albright took her oath of office as secretary of state under President Clinton, she became the first woman to hold that position, and one of the most politically powerful women in the United States—some would say the world. It was a position for which she was well prepared. Secretary Albright had been a research professor of international affairs and the director of the Women in Foreign Service Program at Georgetown University's School of Foreign Service. She had also been America's representative to the United Nations.

As secretary of state, Albright headed a department with many duties. The State Department is responsible for relationships between the United States and other countries. This means that department members must work to strengthen ties between America and its friends, and if these ties become strained, someone in the department has to resolve the issues. If a tense situation in a country vitally important to the United States becomes violent, the department is expected to make recommendations about how to achieve a peaceful resolution. In addition, all foreign diplomats, ambassadors, and embassies are under the secretary's supervision. The State Department has responsibilities at home as well. It oversees the publication of all federal laws and makes sure that all official documents on file are genuine, giving each one that is certified the official seal of the United States.

During Secretary Albright's term, she dealt with many crises. She faced unrest in what was the former Soviet Union, violence in the Balkans and the Middle East, which threatened to spill over into neighboring countries, and an armed struggle with Iraq's leader, Saddam Hussein.

Because being a secretary of state is so demanding, requiring great intelligence, unending energy, and the limitless ability to persuade others to do things they don't want to do, it's no wonder that those who have performed well as secretaries have won the public's approval. In fact, secretaries of state Thomas Jefferson, James Madison, James Monroe, John Quincy Adams, Martin Van Buren, and James Buchanan so impressed Americans that they made each of them president of the United States. By serving her country well,

Madeline Albright helped generate even more confidence in women's ability to deal with complex foreign affairs, creating more opportunities for females to give advice in this demanding field. For example, in 2001, President George W. Bush asked Condoleezza Rice to be his national security advisor. Rice, who had been a professor at Stanford University, vowed to strengthen U.S. military forces and take a strong stand with nations that used threats to achieve their goals. She was the first black woman appointed to this powerful position.

Like Madeleine Albright, Janet Reno was also well prepared for her cabinet position as the first female attorney general. She received her law degree from Harvard University, where she was one of sixteen women in a class of 525. In 1978 she became the first female state attorney in Florida. She was reelected five times. Her office processed, on average, 120,000 cases per year.

Reno quickly learned that the attorney general's position is very demanding. As head of the Department of Justice, the attorney general advises the president about legal issues, represents the United States in court, and makes sure that the laws passed by Congress are enforced. Because there are so many different kinds of laws, the department has many divisions so that each section can specialize. These divisions include the Antitrust Division, which regulates or breaks up businesses that become so large they destroy competition; the Federal Bureau of Investigation (FBI), which catches criminals; and the Drug Enforcement Administration (DEA). The Justice Department also includes the Immigration and Naturalization Service. This division helps immigrants become citizens and deports those who have entered the country illegally.

And finally, besides enforcing laws and advising the president, Reno worked hard as attorney general to make America a better place in which to live. She helped develop programs to keep convicted felons off the streets for long periods of time and to keep children off drugs and away from gangs—major concerns of Americans in all parts of the country.

CHAPTER 8

Running for the Highest Office

I . . . claim the right to speak for the unenfranchised women of the country. . . .I now announce myself as a candidate for the presidency.

—Victoria Woodhull

When Susan B. Anthony cast her ballot in the 1872 election, one of the candidates running for president was Victoria Claflin Woodhull, the first of more than a dozen women to seek the highest office. Woodhull, a stockbroker and publisher, along with her running mate, Frederick Douglass, a former slave, had been nominated by the Equal Rights party. This party had been started by delegates at a National American Woman Suffrage Association convention earlier that year, and its main purpose was to achieve equality for all men and women, a goal Woodhull was especially eager to accomplish. "[All] citizens are entitled to a Constitution to represent them," she said, "and they have got the power to inaugurate it. I do not propose they shall wait sixty years for justice. I want it here and now."[1]

Traditionally, American politics has been dominated by two parties. Because these parties, which have changed throughout our history, have sometimes refused to take a stand on issues that at least some Americans thought vitally important, new organizations were started, often with a lot of fanfare. Known as "third parties," most of these groups existed only for a brief period of time; either the public refused to support them, so they died, or one of the major political parties adopted their cause, and their reason to exist ended.

However, one third party went on to become a major political power. Antislavery Americans banded together in 1854 to start the Republican party. Although its first candidate, John C. Frémont, was defeated in 1856, the Republicans' second candidate, Abraham Lincoln, won the presidency in 1860, a stunning victory for an upstart organization. The Equal Rights party, one of eight third parties in the 1872 election, hoped to duplicate the success of the Republicans.

But even though Victoria Woodhull really believed she could win—she had even selected her outfit for her first day at work—she wasn't a credible candidate. Actually, she fell short in at least three areas. First of all, she faced serious legal problems. She was only thirty-four years old, a year shy of the required age to become president. Also, like fellow suffragist Susan B. Anthony, Woodhull believed that the Fourteenth Amendment gave women the right to vote, so she counted on women marching to the polls in large numbers, casting ballots for her, and then having those ballots tallied. This simply wasn't possible under the laws of the day; every ballot would have been contested.

Second, Woodhull had a questionable professional background for a political candidate. She had been—and probably still was—a medium. At the time, many people were caught up in spiritualism. Kate and Margaret Fox started the trend by announcing that, after hearing strange knocking noises on their bedroom wall, they had made contact with spirits in the next world. When people flocked to the Foxes and paid them to contact dead loved ones, other mediums suddenly appeared, including Woodhull. Most limited

Victoria Claflin Woodhull

their services to simply conversing with spirits. Woodhull not only spoke to the deceased, but she also "cured" patients with her spiritual powers. When the law began to take a dim view of what she and others like her were doing, Victoria left the curing business and invested her considerable profits in stocks.

Third, Woodhull's personal life was not above reproach. She had divorced her first husband, whom she had married when she was fifteen, then married and divorced her second husband, who had been one of her patients—twice. For a while, all three lived in the same house, a situation that caused a lot of gossip.

In addition to her liabilities, Woodhull showed very poor judgment. One week before election day, she ran an article in the newspaper she published, the *Woodhull & Claflin Weekly,* accusing two prominent citizens of committing adultery. She was then charged with distributing obscene material, a federal offense, and she was arrested and put in jail, where she remained until after the election, which, needless to say, she lost.

Even without these handicaps, she would have had a difficult time. Most men were very reluctant to support a female candidate in 1872 (at the next opportunity to do so, only four thousand cast a ballot for a woman), and even if women had voted in large numbers and their votes were counted, many who might have been expected to support her did not. Anthony, for example, objected to a woman campaigning for the presidency then because it took attention away from the suffrage movement. She voted for General U. S. Grant. In a letter she wrote to her friend Elizabeth Cady Stanton, Anthony said, "Well I have been and gone and done it! Positively voted the Republican ticket—straight—this AM at 7 o'clock."[2]

Well aware of Woodhull's debacle, long-established political parties refused to consider a female candidate for the presidency for more than ninety years. Therefore, those who wanted to be president, like Woodhull, turned to third parties. Their causes were varied, as the names of their parties suggest, and there were many election years in which female candidates did not run. The women who did run include:

Belva Lockwood	*National Equal Rights party*	*1884, 1888*
Charlene Mitchell	*Communist party*	*1968*
Linda Jenness	*Socialist Labor party*	*1972*
Margaret Wright	*People's party*	*1976*
Ellen McCormack	*Right to Life party*	*1980*
Maureen Smith	*Peace and Freedom party*	*1980*
Deirdre Griswold	*Workers World party*	*1980*
Sonia Johnson	*Citizens party*	*1984*
Lenora Fulani	*New Alliance party*	*1988, 1992*
Willa Kenoyer	*Socialist party*	*1988*

Helen Halyard	Workers League	1992
Isabell Masters	Looking Back party	1992, 1996, 2000
Gloria La Riva	Workers World party	1992
Mary Cal Hollis	Socialist party	1996
Diane Beall Templin	American party	1996
Marsha Feinland	Peace and Freedom party	1996
Monica Moorehead	Workers World party	1996, 2000

While these women campaigned for third parties, female members of the major political parties began their long struggle for the presidency. In order to win a party's nomination, candidates must enter state primary elections in the spring and early summer of an election year. Anyone may run, and those fortunate enough to win at least some of these primaries, each of which has a certain number of delegates, will be assured of having supporters at the national convention who will nominate and then vote for them.

Presidential campaigns are very expensive; candidates have to run ads, host rallies, and visit many states. Few have enough money of their own to finance such an undertaking, which literally costs millions of dollars, so they turn to supporters for donations. Most party regulars give generously to candidates whose beliefs they share if—and only if—they have a good chance of winning the fall election. No one wants to waste money. Groundbreakers, therefore, have had difficulty raising cash.

Not unexpectedly then, the first three women to enter Republican or Democratic presidential races faced financial problems. In 1964, Margaret Chase Smith, a U.S. senator at the time, challenged Barry Goldwater, who won the Republican nomination but lost the election. In 1972, Representatives Patsy Mink, the first Asian-American woman in Congress, and Shirley Chisholm, the first black female in the House, entered Democratic primaries. Both failed to get the votes needed to win the nomination; George McGovern became the party's nominee. Like Goldwater, he lost the election.

Geraldine Ferraro and Walter Mondale wave to supporters at a rally on July 31, 1984.

More than thirty women have been nominated for vice president. Only one, Geraldine Ferraro, was not a third-party candidate. Ferraro was a hard worker and an ambitious woman. While teaching school, she attended classes at night at Fordham Law School, where she was one of two women in a class of 179. After receiving her degree and being accepted by the New York State Bar in 1961, she joined her husband's real-estate firm. In 1974 she became

The difficulties these women encountered had a powerful effect on another woman who wanted to be president. In early 1988, Representative Patricia Schroeder, also a Democrat, began an all-out effort to raise significant sums of money before officially starting a

an assistant district attorney. A year later, she joined the state's Special Victims Bureau, where she handled cases involving child abuse and rape. At the same time, deeply interested in politics, she became a volunteer in the local Democratic party.

Although Ferraro supported other candidates, when she decided to run for the House in 1978, few volunteered to help her. Instead, she stood on street corners herself to get enough signatures on her petitions that would enable her to run. She not only won that year but was reelected in 1980 and 1982.

In Congress, Ferraro quickly caught the eye of party leaders. She put in extremely long hours and took on tasks no one else wanted to do. When lobbyists pushed for a woman on the 1984 ticket, her name came up repeat-edly, and after Walter Mondale was nominated, he agreed to name Ferraro as his running mate.

The Mondale-Ferraro ticket experienced many problems. Because her position was unique, Ferraro received most of the attention, much of which dwelled on her physical appearance rather than the platform she and Mondale supported. Also, questions about her ability to govern in a crisis dogged her wherever she went, undermining her stature as a worthy candidate and challenging Mondale's decision-making. But even if this issue hadn't been raised, it's unlikely that the Democratic ticket could have been victorious. It was pitted against one of the most popular political pairs in American history, Ronald Reagan and George Bush, who won the election in a landslide.

campaign. When she failed to reach her goal, she tearfully announced that she was scuttling her dream to lead the nation.

Besides money problems, all these women faced discrimination. "I was a black person and I was a woman," Shirley Chisholm said.

"I met far more discrimination as a woman. . . .That was a revelation to me. Black men got together to talk about stopping me. . . . I confronted them. They said I was an intellectual person, that I had the ability, but that this was no place for a woman. If a black person were to run, it should be a man."[3]

Women were discriminated against, in part, because they lacked a military background. Since the American Revolution, the public had often turned to military heroes for president. If the men weren't winners on the battlefield, like Washington, Grant, and Eisenhower, they had at least served in the military. This experience was considered crucial, because the president is the country's commander in chief of the armed forces. But when Bill Clinton, who had not served in the military, became president in 1992, women could no longer be dismissed simply because they hadn't been soldiers.

At the same time, the public claimed that a woman wouldn't be tough enough to lead during a crisis. They pointed to Schroeder's tears as proof. Later, when Secretary of State Madeleine Albright showed her mettle when facing crises in the Balkans and the Middle East, it was clear that a woman could be strong.

Unwilling to let the dream of a female in the Oval Office of the president die and sensing a change in the public's attitude toward female candidates, Republican Elizabeth Dole in 1999 announced that she was running for the presidency. Dole had many assets. Public polls showed that 75 percent of Americans, who were now accustomed to having women in political office, were willing to vote for a qualified female candidate for president. Also, Dole's name was well known. She had served with distinction in two presidential cabinets, and she had been president of the American Red Cross. In addition, her husband, Robert Dole, had run for president in 1996. Even though his effort was unsuccessful, she knew what a presidential campaign entailed.

Although Dole had many strengths, her candidacy was difficult at best. Because female candidates for the presidency are not common, she received a lot of attention from the media. Not all of it was good. Unlike her competitors, her hairstyle and makeup were routinely described, often in unflattering terms. In addition, announcers on the evening news wondered what Robert Dole would be called if his wife were president. First Gentleman? First Spouse? These topics drew attention away from the issues that Elizabeth Dole considered important and contributed to her failure to get her agenda before the public. This in turn undermined her ability to raise money, and she was eventually forced to withdraw from the race.

Even so, the dream of a female president lives on. As more women gain experience on the local and national scene and hone their skills, the chances of Americans electing a female leader—as twenty other nations have done—will increase dramatically. Many political pros believe that day is not far away. Madam President, they say, is in school now, or in a state house, or in Congress, and when she wins, she will change not only American political history but women's lives as well. According to Letty Cottin Pogrebin, who writes about political issues, "On the day that a woman is elected president of the United States, women's voices will break the sound barrier and little girls will hear new music and both will know that from then on, anything they imagine for themselves can become a reality."[4]

CHAPTER 9

The Future

Winning may not be everything, but losing has little to recommend it.

—Dianne Feinstein, U.S. senator 1992–

Clearly, women have had an impact on the political scene. Not only have they voted for more than eighty years, but since 1984, when Geraldine Ferraro ran for vice president, women have cast ballots in larger numbers than men. Usually, but not always—otherwise Ferraro would have won— the majority of these ballots were cast for women, a tradition that began in 1920 and has continued throughout the years. In the 2000 New York senatorial race, for example, 60 percent of the women voting supported First Lady Hillary Rodham Clinton, while in California, 65 percent of the women who cast ballots voted for Dianne Feinstein for senator. If this trend continues, female voters will have a larger impact on future elections than men, and more women will be elected to office.

Just as clearly, female politicians have brought a unique voice to the political scene, introducing issues of great concern to women.

If this trend continues, topics such as abortion, education, welfare, and health care will receive a lot of attention in the coming years.

But even though women have made great progress, female politicians still face a major problem. Unlike trailblazers of the distant past who had to deal with discrimination and naysayers but campaigned before running for office cost a fortune, modern female candidates are generally accepted by the public but hampered by the necessity of raising vast sums of money for a successful campaign. This is especially true for women seeking the highest offices or positions never before held by a female.

Because donations from traditional sources have been meager at best, women have attempted to solve their financial problems by forming political-action committees of their own. Trying to be fair to all, the first committees, which were started in the 1970s, backed as many female candidates as possible, giving a little money to each one who supported women's concerns or the group's goals. While this helped, the amount given was not enough to finance a successful campaign.

In 1984, after watching too many female candidates lose close elections, Ellen Malcolm, a wealthy woman, made up her mind to start a fund that would operate differently. First, she decided to put all her efforts behind a few women who had a good chance to win. Second, she emphasized giving money to cash-strapped candidates as early in their campaigns as possible. She believed that the first money a candidate received was the most important money of all; it helped the would-be politician get off to a good start and, as a result, attracted more donations. "Early money is like yeast," she said, "it makes the 'dough' rise."[1] Malcolm used the first letter of the first five words in her saying to name the group: EMILY's List.

Malcolm was aware that few women had given large sums to a candidate in the past, and large sums were needed. She also knew that most women were not used to asking friends for money. To overcome these problems, she employed practices with which women were comfortable: dues and product parties. First, she rounded up as many like-minded women as she could and charged them an annual fee to join the group. Next, she used a popular party format to raise money. Many women in the 1980s attended gatherings where, after toys, craft materials, or cooking supplies were demonstrated, participants were expected to buy something. Members of EMILY's List held such parties. The "product" was an appearance by the candidate or a representative, and the payment was a contribution toward the campaign fund and the names of other women who would hold or attend another party.

With money in hand, Malcolm and the members of EMILY's List looked about for a candidate who shared their beliefs and looked like a winner. In 1986 they decided to back Barbara Mikulski, a representative from Maryland who wanted to be one of the state's U.S. senators. After winning her party's nomination—with help from the List—Mikulski faced Linda Chavez in the fall election. A blitz of

The always outspoken Barbara Mikulski (left), with help from EMILY's List, ran for a U.S. Senate seat in Maryland in 1986 and won. She is pictured here at a debate with her opponent, Linda Chavez.

expensive statewide television ads turned one of Mikulski's supposedly negative characteristics, her tendency to be a brawler, into an asset. "When it comes to Maryland," she said, beaming with pride, "I'm a fighter."[2] Marylanders loved the ads. Mikulski won 61 percent of the vote in that election, and she has been reelected twice.

Emboldened by the group's success, Malcolm expanded her contacts. By 1998 the organization had 50,000 members who raised $7.5 million. This money was used to help elect seven women to the House. Two years later, the group raised approximately $20 million for female candidates.

EMILY's List is not the only group that supports female candidates. Many organizations raise funds for women and provide volunteers who will make phone calls on behalf of a candidate or go door-to-door to distribute campaign materials. Various groups also provide a forum for candidates to present their beliefs. These organizations include the National Women's Political Caucus, the Latina Political Assembly, the Black Women's Forum, the National Organization for Women, the GOP (Republican) Women's Political Action League, the Women's Leadership Forum, and the Women in the Senate and House (WISH) List. Some groups also provide a forum where elected officials can share their problems and seek advice, hopefully making them top-notch leaders and worthy candidates for reelection.

In short, with ballots in hand, prejudice on the wane, and donations and advice on the rise, the future for women in politics looks brighter than ever. And many would argue that this bright future signals a good thing, for as political appointee Bess Myerson said when addressing a conference of Women in Municipal Government more than twenty years ago, "We need every fine brain . . . every voice with something to say."[3] This hasn't changed. In fact, it is the belief that women have a lot to contribute that keeps female politicians in the running.

TIMELINE

1774 — Fifty-one women in Edenton, North Carolina, sign a statement announcing that they will decide for themselves what actions to take in the political struggle between England and the colonies. This is the first statement of its kind.

1775 — The Revolutionary War begins. Some women seek not only independence from England but political rights for themselves as well.

1848 — The first women's rights convention is held in Seneca Falls, New York. The fight for the ballot for women begins.

1861 — The first shots of the Civil War are fired.

1866 — Elizabeth Cady Stanton runs for the U.S. House of Representatives.

1868 — The Fourteenth Amendment is ratified. U.S. citizens are granted equal protection under the law.

1869 — Susan B. Anthony and Elizabeth Cady Stanton start the National Woman Suffrage Association. Arabella Mansfield, the first woman to be admitted to the legal profession, is accredited by the Iowa bar.

1870	The Fifteenth Amendment is ratified. Black males are enfranchised.
1872	Susan B. Anthony votes in the presidential election. She is arrested in the fall and tried, pronounced guilty, and fined the following year. Victoria Woodhull runs for president, the first woman to do so.
1878	A suffrage amendment is introduced in Congress. It fails.
1890	The National Woman Suffrage Association and the American Woman Suffrage Association merge.
1913	Ida Wells-Barnett starts the Alpha Suffrage Club.
1916	Jeannette Rankin, the first female representative, is elected to the U.S. House. Alice Paul starts the National Woman's Party.
1917	The United States enters World War I.
1920	The Nineteenth Amendment is ratified. Women are enfranchised. Carrie Chapman Catt starts the League of Women Voters. The first all-female town councils are elected in Jackson Hole, Wyoming, and Yoncalla, Oregon.
1922	Rebecca Felton is appointed to the Senate. She is the first female U.S. senator.
1923	Alice Paul's Equal Rights Amendment is introduced in Congress.
1925	Nellie Tayloe Ross is elected governor of Wyoming. She is the first woman to lead a state.
1926	Bertha Knight Landes of Seattle becomes the first female mayor of a large city.
1933	Frances Perkins is appointed secretary of labor. She is the first woman to serve in a president's cabinet.
1934	Florence Ellinwood Allen becomes the first female judge to sit on a federal bench.
1941	The United States enters World War II.

1949	Margaret Chase Smith is elected to the Senate, making her the first woman to serve in both houses of Congress.
1954	The United States begins military action in Vietnam.
1961	Ruth Bader Ginsburg starts the Women's Rights Project.
1964	Patsy Takemoto Mink, the first Asian-American woman elected to the House, takes office. Margaret Chase Smith runs for the presidency. She is the first woman to seek the nomination in a major political party.
1966	Constance Baker Motley becomes the first black woman to be appointed to a federal court.
1968	Shirley Chisholm becomes the first black woman to be elected to the U.S. House.
1970	The Equal Rights Amendment is reintroduced in Congress.
1975	Ella Grasso is elected governor of Connecticut. She is the first woman to become a governor in her own right.
1978	Nancy Kassebaum is elected to the Senate. She is the first woman to serve in this chamber without first having been appointed to political office.
1981	Sandra Day O'Connor, the first female justice, joins the U.S. Supreme Court.
1984	Geraldine Ferraro, the first female vice-presidential candidate of a major political party, runs with Walter Mondale on the Democratic ticket. For the first time, female voters outnumber male voters. EMILY's List is started.
1993	Janet Reno, the first female attorney general of the United States, assumes her duties.
1996	Madeleine Albright, America's first female secretary of state, is appointed to office.
1999	Elizabeth Dole announces her candidacy for the presidency.
2000	Hillary Rodham Clinton is elected to the Senate. She is the first First Lady to run for office.

NOTES

Chapter 1

1. Lynn Sherr, *Failure Is Impossible: Susan B. Anthony in Her Own Words* (New York: Times Books, 1995), p. 115.
2. Sherr, p. 117.

Chapter 2

1. Mary Beth Norton, *Liberty's Daughters: The Revolutionary Experience of American Women 1750–1800* (Boston: Little, Brown, 1980), p. 170.

Chapter 3

1. Sharon Whitney and Tom Raynor, *Women in Politics* (New York: Franklin Watts, 1986), p. 25.
2. Doris Stevens, *Jailed for Freedom: American Women Win the Vote* (Troutdale, OR: NewSage Press, 1995), p. 12.

Chapter 4

1. Clara Bingham, *Women on the Hill: Challenging the Culture of Congress* (New York: Times Books, 1997), p. 21.
2. Bingham, p. 40.
3. Bingham, p. 40.
4. Doris Weatherford, *American Women and World War II* (New York: Facts on File, 1990), p. 30.
5. Shirley Chisholm, *Unbought and Unbossed* (Boston: Houghton Mifflin, 1970), p. 96.
6. Chisholm, p. 97.

7. Karen Foerstel and Herbert N. Foerstel, *Climbing the Hill: Gender Conflict in Congress* (Westport, CT: Praeger, 1996), p. 8.

Chapter 5

1   Sharon Whitney and Tom Raynor, *Women in Politics* (New York: Franklin Watts, 1986), p. 38.
2. "New Hampshire First State with Women in Charge at Statehouse," *Oshkosh Northwestern*, September 11, 1999.
3. Sarah Deutsch, *From Ballots to Breadlines: American Women 1920–1940* (New York: Oxford University Press, 1994), p. 23.
4. Sandra Haarsager, *Bertha Knight Landes of Seattle: Big-City Mayor* (Norman: University of Oklahoma Press, 1994), p. 126.

Chapter 6

1. Carmen Bredeson, *Ruth Bader Ginsburg: Supreme Court Justice* (Springfield, NJ: Enslow Publishers, 1995), p. 7.
2. Bredeson, p. 9.
3. Bredeson, p. 53.
4. Sharon Whitney and Tom Raynor, *Women in Politics* (New York: Franklin Watts, 1986), p. 37.
5. Constance Baker Motley, *Equal Justice Under Law* (New York: Farrar, Straus and Giroux, 1998), p. 226.
6. D. J. Herda, *Sandra Day O'Connor: Independent Thinker* (Springfield, NJ: Enslow Publishers, 1995), p. 46.

Chapter 7

1. Carl Sferrazza Anthony, *America's Most Influential First Ladies* (Minneapolis: Oliver Press, 1992), p. 38.
2. Barbara Silberdick Feinberg, *The Cabinet* (New York: Twenty-First Century Books, 1995), p. 39.

Chapter 8

1. Lois Beachy Underhill, *The Woman Who Ran for President: The Many Lives of Victoria Woodhull* (Bridgehampton, NY: Bridge Works Publishing, 1995), pp. 190, 191.
2. Underhill, p. 232.
3. Eleanor Clift and Tom Brazaitis, *Madam President: Shattering the Last Glass Ceiling* (New York: Scribner, 2000), p. 28.
4. Clift and Brazaitis, pp. 298, 299.

Chapter 9

1. Eleanor Clift and Tom Brazaitis, *Madam President: Shattering the Last Glass Ceiling* (New York: Scribner, 2000), p. 87.
2. Clift and Brazaitis, p. 91.
3. Sharon Whitney and Tom Raynor, *Women in Politics* (New York: Franklin Watts, 1986), p. 123.

BIBLIOGRAPHY

Abraham, Henry J. *Justices, Presidents, and Senators: A History of the U.S. Supreme Court Appointments from Washington to Clinton.* Lanham, MD: Rowman & Littlefield, 1999.

Anderson, Paul. *Janet Reno: Doing the Right Thing.* New York: John Wiley, 1994.

Anthony, Carl Sferrazza. *America's Most Influential First Ladies.* Minneapolis: Oliver Press, 1992.

Bingham, Clara. *Women on the Hill: Challenging the Culture of Congress.* New York: Times Books, 1997.

Bredeson, Carmen. *Ruth Bader Ginsburg: Supreme Court Justice.* Springfield, NJ: Enslow Publishers, 1995.

Burrell, Barbara. *Public Opinion, the First Ladyship, and Hillary Rodham Clinton.* New York: Garland Publishing, 1997.

Chisholm, Shirley. *Unbought and Unbossed.* Boston: Houghton Mifflin, 1970.

Clift, Eleanor, and Tom Brazaitis. *Madam President: Shattering the Last Glass Ceiling.* New York: Scribner, 2000.

Deutsch, Sarah. *From Ballots to Breadlines: American Women, 1920–1940.* New York: Oxford University Press, 1994.

Feinberg, Barbara Silberdick. *The Cabinet*. New York: Twenty-First Century Books, 1995.

Foerstel, Karen, and Herbert N. Foerstel. *Climbing the Hill: Gender Conflict in Congress*. Westport, CT: Praeger, 1996.

Haarsager, Sandra. *Bertha Knight Landes of Seattle: Big-City Mayor*. Norman: University of Oklahoma Press, 1994.

Herda, D. J. *Sandra Day O'Connor: Independent Thinker*. Springfield, NJ: Enslow Publishers, 1995.

Motley, Constance Baker. *Equal Justice Under Law*. New York: Farrar, Straus and Giroux, 1998.

"New Hampshire First State with Women in Charge at Statehouse." *Oshkosh Northwestern*, September 11, 1999.

Norton, Mary Beth. *Liberty's Daughters: The Revolutionary Experience of American Women 1750–1800*. Boston: Little, Brown, 1980.

Pollack, Jill S. *Women on the Hill: A History of Women in Congress*. New York: Franklin Watts, 1996.

Preimesberger, Jon, ed. *National Party Conventions*. Washington, D.C.: Congressional Quarterly, 1995.

Sherr, Lynn. *Failure Is Impossible: Susan B. Anthony in Her Own Words*. New York: Times Books, 1995.

Southwick, Leslie H. *Presidential Also-Rans and Running Mates, 1788 Through 1996*. Jefferson, NC: McFarland, 1998.

Stevens, Doris. *Jailed for Freedom: American Women Win the Vote*. Troutdale, OR.: NewSage Press, 1995.

Underhill, Lois Beachy. *The Woman Who Ran for President: The Many Lives of Victoria Woodhull*. Bridgehampton, NY: Bridge Works, 1995.

Wallace, Patricia Ward. *Politics of Conscience: A Biography of Margaret Chase Smith*. Westport, CT: Praeger, 1995.

Weatherford, Doris. *American Women and World War II*. New York: Facts on File, 1990.

Whitney, Sharon, and Tom Raynor. *Women in Politics*. New York: Franklin Watts, 1986.

FURTHER READING

There are numerous biographies about many of the women mentioned in this text. For more information, check out: *Susan B. Anthony: Voice for Women's Voting Rights* by Martha Kendall (Enslow, 1997); *Eleanor Roosevelt: A Life of Discovery* by Russell Freedman (Clarion, 1993); *Elizabeth Dole: Public Servant* by Carolyn Mulford (Enslow, 1992); *Frances Perkins: A Member of the Cabinet* by Bill Severn (Hawthorn Books, 1976); and *Justice Sandra Day O'Connor* by Mary Virginia Fox (Enslow, 1983).

Two excellent collective biographies about women in politics are Laurie Lindop's *Political Leaders* (Twenty-First Century Books, 1996) and Charles Gulotta's *Extraordinary Women in Politics* (Children's Press, 1998). Lindop's book has sections on Janet Reno and Geraldine Ferraro. Gulotta's book includes female political leaders from all over the world, including many who have served in the U.S. Congress.

The Encyclopedia of Women in Politics, edited by Jeffrey D. Schultz and Laura van Assendelft (Oryx Press, 1999), has detailed information about the political scene. It is an excellent reference book.

Another excellent source of information is the Internet. The Center for American Women and Politics at Rutgers University provides data about women in office now and in the past. Readers can get either a national report or a state-by-state accounting. Simply type "CAWP" in your search engine to make the connection. For state reports, click on "The Facts" at the top of the page. When the page changes, click on "State by State," located at the left of the screen. Also, almost every woman who is in office has her own Web site. To learn more about her and her agenda, type the politician's name in your search engine. Many sources have also set up Web sites about women who have held office in the past. Again, simply enter the woman's name. An amazing number of sites will pop up, making it easy to learn a lot more about women in politics.

INDEX

Page numbers in *italics* refer to illustrations.

Able, Hazel, 50
Abzug, Bella, *47*
Adams, John Quincy, 84
African-American women, 45, 46–48, *47*, 51, 73, 82, 89, 91–92
Albright, Madeleine, 82–84, 92
Allen, Florence Ellinwood, 70–72
Allen, Maryon, 50
American Civil Liberties Union (ACLU), 69–70
American Revolution, 18
American Woman Suffrage Association, 25–26
Anthony, Susan B., 9–11, *12*, 13, 20, 23, 25, 26, 30, 37, 75, 85, 86, 88
Antislavery movement, 19, 23, 37
Asian-American women, 45–46, *46*, 89

Babbitt, Bruce, 74
Barker, Penelope, 15–17, 54
Black suffrage movement, 35–38
Blackwell, Alice Stone, 65
Boggs, Corrine, 48
Bowring, Eva, 50

Boxer, Barbara, 51, 52, 53, 68
Bradwell v. Illinois (1873), 68
Brown v. Board of Education of Topeka, Kansas (1954), 66, 72
Buchanan, James, 84
Burger, Warren, *74*
Burt, Mary, *62*
Bush, George, 66, 91
Bushfield, Vera, 50
Byrne, Jane, 63

Cabinet members, 79–84
Caraway, Hattie, 49
Carnahan, Jean, 54
Carnahan, Mel, 54
Catt, Carrie Chapman, 29–31, *31*, 35
Catt, George, 30
Chao, Elaine, 82
Chapman, Leo, 30
Chavez, Linda, 97, 97–98
Chisholm, Shirley, *37*, 45, 46–48, 89, 91–92
Civil Rights Movement, 38, 45, 72
Civil War, 10, 23, 24, *25*
Clinton, Bill, *51*, 79, 83, 92

Clinton, Chelsea, *51*
Clinton, Hillary Rodham, *51*, 51, 79, 95
Collins, Martha Layne, 60
Colonial period, 15–17
Constitution of the United States, 10, 18, 24, 25, 30, 32–37, 39, 66, 70, 71, 86
Cox, James, 42
Crowley, Richard, 10

Dole, Elizabeth, *12*, 13, 81, 92–93
Dole, Robert, *12*, 92–93
Douglas, Stephen A., 77
Douglass, Frederick, 85

Eastland, James, 72–73
Edenton Tea Party, *16*, 16–17
Edwards, Elaine, 50
Eisenhower, Dwight, 82, 92
EMILY's List, 96–98
Employment of women, 24, 30, 32, 69–70
Equal Rights Amendment (ERA), 32, 45, 49, 74

Feinland, Marsha, 89
Feinstein, Dianne, 51, 63, 95
Felton, Rebecca, 49, 54
Ferguson, James "Pa," *58*, 59
Ferguson, Miriam Amanda "Ma," 57, 58, 58–59
Ferraro, Geraldine, *90*, 90–91, 95
Fifteenth Amendment to the Constitution, 35–37
Fillmore, Millard, 10
Finney, Joan, 61
First Ladies, 77–79
Fourteenth Amendment, 10, 35, 37, 66, 70, 86
Franklin, Barbara H., 82
Frémont, John C., 86
Frontiero, Sharon, 70
Frontiero v. Richardson (1973), 70
Fulani, Lenora, 88

Gage, Matilda Joslyn, 20
George III, King of England, 15, 17
Ginsburg, Ruth Bader, 69–70, 75
Goldwater, Barry, 89
Governors, 57–61
Grant, Ulysses S., 88, 92
Grasso, Ella, 60
Graves, Dixie, 50
Great Depression, 78
Griswold, Deidre, 88

Halyard, Helen, 89
Harding, Florence, 77
Harding, Warren G., 42
Hardwick, Thomas W., 49
Harris, Patricia, 82
Hawkins, Paula, 50
Heckler, Margaret, 48, 82
Herman, Alexis, 81–82
Hill, Anita, 67
Hills, Carla, 82
History of Woman Suffrage, A (Stanton, Anthony, and Gage), 20
Hobby, Oveta Culp, 82
Hollingworth, Beverly, 61
Hollis, Mary Cal, 89
Hollister, Nancy, 61
House of Representatives, 34, 39–48, 52–53, 60
Huck, Winnifred Sprague Mason, 44
Hufstedler, Shirley M., 82
Hull, Jane Dee, 61
Humphrey, Muriel, 50
Hunt, Ward, 10, 11

Jefferson, Thomas, 83
Jenness, Linda, 88
Johnson, Lyndon B., 72
Johnson, Nancy, 48
Johnson, Sonia, 88
Judges, 70–75

Kahn, Florence P., 44
Kaptur, Marcy, 48
Kassebaum, Nancy, 50–51

Kassebaum, Philip, 50
Kenoyer, Willa, 88
King, Martin Luther, Jr., 38
Kreps, Juanita, 82
Kunin, Madeleine, 60

Landes, Bertha Knight, 63
Landon, Alf, 50
La Riva, Gloria, 89
League of Women Voters, 30, 35, 60
Legal profession, 65–75
Lincoln, Abraham, 77–78, 80, 86
Lincoln, Mary Todd, 77–78
Literacy tests, 37–38
Lockwood, Belva, 88
Long, Rose, 50

Madison, James, 83–84
Malcolm, Ellen, 96–98
Mansfield, Arabella, 68
Marshall, Thurgood, 66
Martin, Lynn, 81
Martz, Judy, 61
Masters, Isabell, 89
Mayors, 63
McCarthy, Joseph, 52
McCormack, Ellen, 88
McCorvey, Norma, 69
McGovern, George, 89
McLaughlin, Ann Dore, 81
Mikulski, Barbara, 52, 53, 97, 97–98
Mink, Patsy Takemoto, 45–46, *46*, 89
Minner, Ruth, 61
Mitchell, Charlene, 88
Mofford, Rose, 60
Mondale, Walter, *90*, 90, 91
Monroe, James, 84
Moorehead, Monica, 89
Moseley-Braun, Carol, 51
Motley, Constance Baker, 70, 72–73
Mott, Lucretia, 19, 21
Mullins, Rita, 55
Murray, Patty, 51
Myerson, Bess, 98

National American Woman Suffrage
    Association (NAWSA), 26, 27,
    29–32, 34, 35, 85
National Association of Colored
    Women, 37
National League of Women Voters
    (*see* League of Women Voters)
National Woman's Party (NWP), 29,
    31–35, 37
National Woman Suffrage Associa-
    tion, 20, 25, 26
Neuberger, Maureen, 50
Nineteenth Amendment to the Con-
    stitution, 30, 32–35, 37, 39, 71
Nolan, Mae Ella, 44
Norton, Gale, 82
Nursing, 24, *25*

Oakar, Mary Rose, 48
O'Connor, John, 73, *74*
O'Connor, Sandra Day, 70, 73–75, *74*
O'Leary, Hazel, 82
Olmstead, Roy, 63
Orr, Kay, 60

Paul, Alice, 29, 31–32, *33*, 45
Pearson, James, 50
Perkins, Frances, *80*, 80–81
Pogrebin, Letty Cottin, 93
Poll tax, 37
Presidential advisers, 77–84
Presidential candidates, 13, 85–93
Presidential elections
    1872, 9, 10, 85–88
    1920, 39, 42
    1964, 89
    1972, 89
Progressive Era, 26
Pyle, Gladys, 50

Quakers, 19

Rankin, Jeannette, 40–44, *41*, 48,
    52, 54
Ray, Dixie Lee, 60

Reagan, Ronald, 52, 73, 74, 91
Rehnquist, William, 73
Reno, Janet, 82–84
Richards, Ann, 61
Roberts, Barbara, 61
Robertson, Alice Mary, 42–44, *43*
Roe v. Wade (1973), 69
Rogers, Edith Nourse, 44–45, 48, 82
Roosevelt, Eleanor, 78, *78*–79, 81
Roosevelt, Franklin D., 42, 71, 78,
     78–81
Ross, Nellie Tayloe, *57*, 57–58
Ross, William, 57, 58
Roukema, Marge, 48

School desegregation, 66
Schroeder, Patricia, 3, 48, 90–92
Selden, Henry R., 10–11
Senate, 34, 39, 45, 49–54, 66–68,
     71, 75
Seneca Falls Convention (1848), 21,
     23
Severyns, William, 63
Sexual harassment, 67
Shaheen, Jeanne, 61
Shalala, Donna E., 82
Sheppard-Towner Maternity and
     Infancy Aid bill, 42–44
Shuler, Nettie Rogers, 35
Slavery, 19, 21, 23–24, 36
Smith, Margaret Chase, 49, 50, 52,
     89
Smith, Maureen, 88
Smith, Virginia, 48
Snowe, Olympia, 52, 53
Stanton, Elizabeth Cady, *19*, 19–21,
     39–40, 88
Stanton, Harriot, *19*
Stanton, Henry Brewster, 20
State and local government, 55–63
State legislatures, 61–62
Stone, Lucy, 25–26
Supreme Court of the United States,
     65–69, 72–75

Swift, Jane, 61
Sytek, Donna, 61–62

Templin, Diane Beall, 89
Third parties, 86, 88–89
Thirteenth Amendment to the Con-
     stitution, 24
Thomas, Clarence, 66–68
Title IX Education Act of 1972, 45
Town boards (councils), 56, 62–63
Triangle Shirtwaist Company fire, 81
Truth, Sojourner, 36

Van Buren, Martin, 84
Veneman, Ann, 82
Vietnam War, 45, 47, 48
Violence Against Women Act, 53

Wade, Henry, 69
Wallace, George, 59
Wallace, Lurleen, 59
Walsh, Debbie, 39
Walton, Thomas, 49
Washington, George, 18, 79, 92
Weddington, Sarah, 69
Wells-Barnett, Ida B., 37
Whitman, Christine Todd, 61
Whitmire, Kathy, 63
Wilkinson, Eliza, 15
Wilson, Woodrow, 33, 40, 41
Woman's Bible, The (Stanton), 20
Women's Loyal National League,
     23–24
Women's Rights Project, 70
Women's suffrage movement, 9–11,
     20, 21, 23–38, *27*, *28*–29
Woodhull, Victoria Claflin, 85–88, *87*
World Anti-Slavery Convention
     (1840), 21
World War I, 30–31, 40–41
World War II, 42, 45, 52, '78
Wright, Margaret, 88

Yoncalla, Oregon, *62*, 62–63